JAPAN

edited by

KENNETH A. GROSSBERG

Philadelphia **ISHI** *A Publication of the*
INSTITUTE FOR THE STUDY OF HUMAN ISSUES

TODAY

Manufactured in the United States of America

Japan Today symbol by Kuan Chang

Designed by Adrianne Onderdonk Dudden

Library of Congress Cataloging in Publication Data

Main entry under title:

Japan today.

    Based on panel discussions in the "Japan
Today" program held in 1979 in several American
cities.
    1. Japan—Civilization—1945–   —Addresses,
essays, lectures.   I. Grossberg, Kenneth A.
DS822.5.J4   952.04   81–1077
ISBN 0–89727–018–5   AACR2
ISBN 0–89727–019–3 (pbk.)

For information, write:

Director of Publications
ISHI
3401 Science Center
Philadelphia, Pennsylvania 19104
U.S.A.

Preface

April 1979 saw the launching of what may well be the largest celebration ever of the people and culture of one nation by another nation—a tribute to a friend. Under the general canopy of "Japan Today," this celebration was a three-month program presenting concurrent events in seven American cities. Americans were able as never before to enjoy a concentrated and kaleidoscopic view of Japan through a well-integrated series of panel discussions; films; art, craft, and technology exhibitions; performances of Japanese music, dance, and drama; courses, workshops, lectures, and numerous special events. Museums, art galleries, movie houses, and various institutions in each of the seven cities hosted these events. "Japan Today" was a credit to the enormous efforts of the Japan Society in New York, and the Smithsonian Resident Associate Program and Meridian House International in Washington, D.C., of the benefactors who made it financially possible, and of the hundreds of people on both sides of the Pacific whose intellectual and artistic contributions made it such a resounding success.

At the center of this rich variety of offerings was a series of panel discussions whose participants met in turn in Washington, New York, Chicago, and Denver. (Other lecture series were offered in Boston, Los Angeles, and Miami.) The organizers of "Japan Today" thought it only fitting that there be some concrete record of these panel discussions so that some of the atmosphere and the knowledge disseminated in the course of the panelists' journey across the United States could be preserved. An American presider and a commentator were engaged in each of the four cities, and discussions and emphases varied, often widely, from locale to locale. The very dynamism of the panel format presents a problem for capturing that atmosphere between the covers of a book. In addition to formal presentations, the discussants' comments and the panelists' answers to audience questions were also of interest. This book is an attempt to preserve in capsule form some of the intellectual excitement of those panel discussions and to capture the spontaneity of opinion as well as the more structured lecture presentations. To provide more focus than is possible in a series of panel discussions involving eighteen panelists and extending over six weeks, I have chosen to use only representative examples of the papers; forewords to the parts provide a setting for treating the informal remarks and those papers I have not been able to include.

The ten papers reproduced in full constitute less than half of the wealth of material revealed in the course of "Japan Today." My one regret is that the limitations of a single book prevent the unabridged inclusion of every speech delivered.

Each of the eighteen Japanese panelists, most of whom came from Japan especially for this purpose, made a substantial contribution to our understanding of Japan today. The names of the participants and of the discussants mentioned in the text are listed in the Appendix. It is sincerely hoped that this book will serve to whet the reader's appetite to explore other works on Japan by these authors and by others.

New York   Kenneth A. Grossberg

Contents

Acknowledgments

The inspiration and initiative for "Japan Today" came from the National Endowment for the Humanities. The initial funding came jointly from the National Endowments for the Arts and Humanities, with a generous grant from Matsushita Electric (Panasonic) almost doubling the original funds. The Japan Foundation and the Japan–U.S. Friendship Commission supported specific portions of the national program. These major grants were supplemented in each of the seven participating cities by contributions from dozens of organizations. Our gratitude is extended to all who helped make "Japan Today" possible.

Organizing and coordinating a program of the scope and size of "Japan Today" was immensely challenging, involving more than 180 organizations and hundreds of people, as well as the governments of both countries. The Japan Society, Meridian House International, and the Smithsonian Resident Associate Program designed the program, with the Japan Society acting as national coordinator. Each city had a local coordinator who, working with an advisory committee, drew on elements of the national program and on local resources to create a version of "Japan Today" which would interest and stimulate the audience.

On the national level, certain elements of the program, including the film series and several performing arts events, traveled to more than one city. Among these, the series of six panel discussions provided a special intellectual excitement and an opportunity for the public to interact with eminent Japanese thinkers and doers. The National Endowment for the Humanities and Matsushita Electric took a direct interest in the panel discussions, and it is with their support that this book has been published. Kenneth Grossberg has risen to the challenge of weaving out of the transcripts of six panels in four cities a coherent introduction to the subtlety of contemporary Japanese thought and culture. He has preserved the integrity of the speakers' presentations while at the same time distilling their observations, impressions, and insights to meet the limitations of space—and always with gracious prose. Sandra Faux, Director of Publications at the Japan Society, has also played a vital role in the planning of this book.

Each panelist has had an opportunity to review and approve the report of his or her remarks printed here. To them go our deepest thanks for taking the time to travel across the United States to share their perceptions of the complexity and vitality of Japanese society and culture today with a broad cross-section of Americans.

This book does not aim to explain contemporary Japanese society, economics, politics, foreign policy, or life-styles. Rather, it hopes to stimulate interest, to provoke in the reader a desire to know more about a country whose goals may be the same as ours, yet whose ways of arriving at them are vastly different from our own.

David MacEachron
Project Director, and
President, Japan Society

Joseph John Jova
President
Meridian House
International

Janet Solinger
Director
Smithsonian Resident
Associate Program

Virginia Petree
Project Coordinator
"Japan Today"

Introduction
KENNETH A. GROSSBERG

Despite its title, *Japan Today* is really a book about Japan tomorrow. All the issues discussed in this book—cultural, political, economic, and social—are concerned to a greater or lesser extent with the future, and with Japan's place in that future. The papers presented here are only a sampling of what was surely the most comprehensive and far-reaching program on Japan ever undertaken anywhere outside that country. By the very scale of the effort, the "Japan Today" symposia made an important statement about Japan's role in the contemporary world, but they also served to elicit a new interest about Japan in the United States. Whatever the motivation for this interest—curiosity, admiration, a heightened sense of competition—the net result was what you find in this volume: a multidimensional examination of the attitudes, institutions, arts, and social behavior of one of the world's most fascinating nations. Such lavish attention is by no means misplaced, for probably no other people can so provide a mirror, a reflection, of our own inscrutable American society. It is not that the Japanese are so different from us, since in many respects they are not, or that they are so much like us, since in certain ways they could not be more different. It is rather that the *combination* of similarities and dissimilarities with American society is so unique in Japan that they can help us to understand ourselves simply by our observing them.

In a way, the eminent Japanese authorities who con-

tributed to this volume are themselves examples of one of
the most distinctive Japanese traits, namely, preoccupation
with defining and understanding the essence of what it
means to be Japanese. All nations clutch to their collective
bosoms a cherished notion of what they are and what they
wish foreigners to think of them, and yet the Japanese seem
to be in a class by themselves in this respect, because they
are at one and the same time unbelievably ethnocentric and
extraordinarily cosmopolitan. Every Japanese, it seems, has
what he or she believes to be a crystal-clear image of what
being Japanese is all about, and will expound at great length
to captive audiences of foreigners on the subject, often con-
tradicting one another in their endeavor to get at the core of
"Japaneseness." On the other hand, probably no other people on earth are better equipped emotionally or intellectually
for appreciating a foreign culture on its own terms. The
Japanese have an uncanny ability to grasp the finer points of
the art, music, and literature created by foreigners, and they
are among the most sophisticated audiences in the world.
This has been attested to by such diverse artists as opera
singers and jazz percussionists. It is almost ironic that the
Japanese are so *au courant* in foreign cultures (and by this I do
not mean only Western cultures) that they can grasp their
essence with little trouble, whereas it is still so hard for them
to agree among themselves about what the essence of their
own culture is. This paradox underlies much of the success
—and the failure—that Japan has met with in the past, and
the prospects which confront that nation in the future. (In
this volume Akira Iriye and Yoshikazu Sakamoto present
their views on the puzzle that is Japanese identity.)

   Among the issues that today loom most salient for Japan
are those of home, work, governance, and life-style. The
home is of course the epicenter for all these problems, and
the place where people feel them most intensely if not most

consciously. One such issue involves the social definition of male and female in present-day urban society. Rapidly changing attitudes toward sexual stereotyping of male and female roles are abetted by the almost total absence of the wage-earning father from the average urban middle-class family during waking hours, as well as by a growing predominance of women as teachers in elementary and junior high schools, and the general irrelevance of gender to performing well in the majority of jobs available in an advanced technological society. In other words, the trauma of modernization has hit Japan with full force, and not too much later than it hit American society, with similar alienating and promising consequences. This is but one of the many paradoxes of Japanese life dealt with in this volume, and Sumiko Furuya Iwao's article (Part 1) indicates that her people are making their peace with this radical change in the same flexible manner that has characterized their adaptation in other areas. Aging and the aged, as Kaoru Kobayashi points out (Part 1), is another area of social change that demands imaginative solutions.

When we look at Japanese culture it becomes apparent that this is not the first time allegedly revolutionary social and economic changes have occurred in Japan. What seems on the surface to be an unprecedented development may in reality turn out to be a recurrence of a previously existing phenomenon. Take the examples given by Masakazu Yamazaki (Part 3) concerning the sociability of the Japanese before the seventeenth century. The Japanese are characterized as having been gregarious, informal, spontaneous, and quite unlike the more recent stereotype that depicts them as reserved, sober, stiff, and diffident. The drastic change in their public social behavior has been attributed to the severity of the Tokugawa regime, and most Japanese now accept the view of themselves as shy and brittle as their natural state. This just shows how recent the origin of a hallowed "tradition" may be, with the past situation in fact resembling the present more than an intermediate stage resembles either one. Kazuko Tsurumi (Part 3), on the other hand, demonstrates how tradition—in this case Shinto religious tradition —was used as a pretext for implementing certain very modern forms of political authoritarianism. She also indicates, however, that if given half a chance the benign and tolerant faces of these traditions can easily reassert themselves. Perhaps it is the very inability of Japanese to agree among themselves concerning the nature of Japanese tradition which preserves that tradition as a living, evolving entity. Where they do manage to agree, or where they set up authorities as arbiters of that tradition, spontaneity and creativity often disappear.

One factor influencing Japanese culture is affluence. There is no doubt that the so-called economic miracle has had an enormous impact on the direction cultural and social developments have taken during the last three decades. It is understandable that pundits have dubbed this period the "Showa Genroku," for not since the Genroku period in the late seventeenth century has Japan enjoyed such an explosion of wealth and conspicuous consumption. "Showa" refers to the era name of the present reigning emperor. Whether expressed or not, the social problems, the leisure boom, the conflicts of sexual roles felt by both women and men, the national identity crisis, and so on are all affected by this unprecedented affluence. Yotaro Kobayashi (Part 4) discusses the nuts and bolts of business in a Japan now awash in this affluence. But now Japanese society is experiencing the first shocks—"Nixon shocks" and otherwise—of the realization that such affluence may not continue unabated. Nixon's floating of the dollar resulted in a greatly strengthened yen, which made Japan's success all too conspicuous to be suffered in silence by her greatest economic competitors. But Japan has also been shaken by the unending upward spiral of fuel prices. Having been used to poverty and scarcity on a scale much greater than that familiar to most Americans, the Japanese now may well become world leaders in solving the spiritual as well as the material problems spawned by the new austerity. For this reason, a number of people, including Ezra Vogel, who was a discussant at the panels, are urging us to learn from Japan what we can in areas of human endeavor and social organization where Japanese have proven the worthiness of their approach. It may well be that, in order to preserve the individual's standard of living and even political freedom in the world of the future, other nations might consider some of the limitations Japan's society imposes on the egotism of its members.

At the root of all this lie the economy and the political system. Interdependence in the world market, and the critical energy shortage and its attendant diplomatic tensions, have rendered Japan's desire to retain its semi-autonomous position increasingly problematic. The United States and Europe are demanding freer access to the lucrative Japanese domestic market, while many Japanese echo Eisuke Sakakibara's sentiments (Part 4) that American firms do not try hard enough to penetrate that market. All the rhetoric notwithstanding, both sides are beginning to realize the necessity for talking to—not at—each other. Perhaps no two nations have as much to lose from mutual recriminations and resentment as the United States and Japan, and fortunately both seem to realize this fact.

If the economic links are beset with difficulties, the political arena is deceptively quiescent. The only item that all commentators like Tasuku Asano (Part 5) can agree upon is that the so-called "postwar era" in Japanese politics, with its attendant stability and Liberal Democratic Party domination of the national Diet, may be ending. It is much harder to arrive at a consensus concerning the future, and we must wait and see whether Kan Ori's optimism (Part 5) or Asano's doubts will be confirmed by political developments. Pending are arguments concerning the country's national security, which range all the way from the proposal that Japan stockpile nuclear weapons to the suggestion by one Japanese analyst that the country should simply surrender if attacked by the Soviet Union. In other words, Japan, which has not had to think about the unthinkable since its defeat in 1945, must now accept the political responsibility of being a power with enormous economic clout. This is a difficult adjustment for a nation that has grown accustomed to thinking of itself as the weak pawn of external political forces, emanating primarily from the United States but also from the oil-rich states and the Soviet Union. It is obvious, however, that Japan can persist in the notion of its own passivity only at the risk of antagonizing present allies. One wonders if those other nations will be any happier once Japan begins to seize the political initiative, since the Japanese perception of national interest is not always identical to that of her Western allies.

Internally, Japan is engaged in an ongoing conflict sparked by those who wish to establish the primacy of the individual's rights in a society that has tended to value more highly the collective will. There have been significant achievements in this regard during the past thirty years, but recession and a mood of austerity threaten the political and social latitude of the individual in Japan as elsewhere. More than most nations, Japan has dealt effectively with many of the technical problems of postindustrial society, such as mass transit and the quality of life, and even the severe overcrowding of the Tokyo metroplex is relieved by pedestrian malls closed to traffic. The deeper psychological toll of modern urban society is no less severe in Japan than elsewhere, however, and it is in this area that some of Japan's traditional institutions and customs may come to her aid to redress the balance and preserve a semblance of stability for the future.

Due to their largely visual nature, the presentations in the panel on issues of urban society could not be included in this volume, although some points made by the participants deserve mention. Japan is a quintessentially urbanized nation, and has been for longer than most countries. Although one of the panelists, Fumihiko Maki, commented that historically the Japanese have not resorted to large-scale rational planning, one could argue that as far back as the sixteenth century the castle town *(jōkamachi)* was a monument to urban planning. It is true, as discussant Tetsuo Najita pointed out, that the governing principle in the design of those castle towns was to make them impregnable to attack by confusing an enemy with labyrinthine streets, and perhaps this is what Maki referred to as a "nondeductive" approach. Maki raised another issue that also explains the nature of the urban landscape: Japanese are more attached to the land than they are to edifices, an unusual attitude, given the fact that the population now overwhelmingly inhabits large cities. But it does help to perpetuate the villagelike atmosphere of neighborhoods in a city like Tokyo by serving as a link to the attitudes of rural communities with which most urban Japanese now have only limited contact. Japan may provide us with some of the answers to our own urban problems. Another panel discussant, Robert Reischauer, indicated that American urban problems are quite distinct from Japan's, but it does seem that our largest conurbations could benefit from adapting some of Japan's solutions in areas such as mass transit, crime control, and pedestrian-traffic patterning.

The lesson throughout "Japan Today" seems as clear in this area as in all the others: the age of Japan as follower and imitator, if it ever were even partially true, is no more. Japan today is one of the world's most creative and innovative societies, and that is no small collateral with which to face the future.

1

The Japanese Today: Changing Life-Patterns

Foreword

Since Ruth Benedict wrote *The Chrysanthemum and the Sword,* we have grown accustomed to thinking of Japan in terms of dichotomies. In the first "Japan Today" panel, panelist Masao Kunihiro referred to them as "contradictory notions," which include the following paired opposites: egalitarian/nonegalitarian, democratic/nondemocratic, vertical/anti-hierarchical, materialistic/spiritual, affluent/impoverished, traditional/innovative, religious/secular, aesthetic/insensitive, and internationally-minded/ethnocentric. These dichotomies formed the basis for much of the dialogue concerning Japan's changing life-patterns. Many participants concluded that Japan really comprises a unity of opposites, or, as Kunihiro put it, that Japan is a "non-Aristotelian both/and" culture, rather than an "either/or" culture. Of course, Japan is not the only society that can be so categorized, and yet the unity of the great extremes that exist there would seem to give Japan a unique place among nations. In this part, panelist Sumiko Iwao accentuates that uniqueness by asking us to think about America's territorial size and population in Japanese terms, so that we can comprehend the effects of extreme demographic and geographic pressures on Japanese behavior.

In addition to the view which sees Japanese culture in terms of paradox and contradiction, there is an equally popular school of thought reflected in the stress Kunihiro placed on the amazing continuity of Japanese social structure and ways of thinking—this in spite of the great changes that have engulfed that country during the past thirty years. At the same time, Kunihiro doubted some of the most cherished stereotypes held about Japanese, such as their homogeneity. While Japanese are very homogeneous racially and linguistically, he cautioned, we must not forget that they are also highly compartmentalized into different social segments, in what Masao Maruyama, critic and Professor of Political Science at Tokyo University, called an "octopus-pot culture." The image is a novel one, but the analogy is useful: when there is little interchange between segments of the society, cross-fertilization of ideas is often absent.

Kunihiro also pleaded, as do many of his countrymen, that Japan's affluence is partly illusory, because it is a resource-poor land and must generate huge amounts of export business to keep its large middle class afloat. He cited a survey conducted at Sophia University in Tokyo, in which many college students registered the opinion that they would never be able to own their own homes. But such evidence may actually support the notion that Japan is now affluent enough to participate in the problems of distribution being experienced by all advanced nations. Arguing that Japan is indeed quite affluent, discussant Ezra Vogel noted that Japan exceeded even the most outlandish predictions of futurologists like Herman Kahn. Early in the 1970s, Kahn forecast that Japan would catch up to the United States in income per capita by 1985; in fact, this happened as early as 1978.

Another cherished stereotype is that the Japanese are a harmonious people, and analysts refer to the power of the group over the individual in supporting arguments to this effect. Discussant Solomon Levine was not sure that such a generalization can stand unqualified when, in fact, probably a larger percentage of the working population in Japan participates in strikes than in any other country in the world.

Indeed, the group model has itself metamorphosed: despite the pretense of harmony, Levine asserted that the ability to say "no" nineteen different ways in Japanese (including saying "yes" when one means "no") reveals that a good deal of tension must underlie the social harmony. Iwao refers specifically to emerging tensions where women are concerned, and there are many other areas, such as the problems of the elderly, where conflict is known to exist.

For example, the issue of seniority and job security is intimately linked to that of Japan's rapidly aging population, as panelist Kaoru Kobayashi's contribution makes clear. It has been predicted that by the year 2000 one out of every five Japanese will be over sixty years of age, and only three out of five will be at the "productive" ages between fifteen and fifty-nine. With people living longer and yet still forced to retire at a fairly young age, Japanese society has not yet accommodated the growing numbers of elderly who can no longer depend on their children to the extent that previous generations were able. Less than ten years ago, then Prime Minister Satō asserted that care of the aged was the responsibility of their children and not that of public agencies and the government. To many Japanese this opinion now seems callous and misguided, and there is every reason to believe that Japan will not abandon its senior citizens to the vagaries of a shifting family structure but will develop new mechanisms for utilizing their talents and energies toward productive ends. Among other things, the compulsory age of retirement will be raised gradually, and some companies have even initiated plans to employ senior citizens in factories, where they would perform jobs of a skilled and semiskilled nature.

It is remarkable that social life in Japan remains as orderly as it does, in spite of the fact that the extended family has given way to the nuclear family as the typical domestic setting. The answer may lie partly in the types of roles played

within that nuclear unit. Both Vogel and Iwao have emphasized the social rewards given to the Japanese woman who
spends her time mothering, and the resulting benefit in time
and attention given to the basic needs of children. This is in
sharp contrast to the situation that prevails in American
society today, where a woman tends to feel apologetic for
being a housewife. There is some question as to how much
longer the Japanese mother can continue to devote so much
of her time to her children. Women currently make up one-
third of Japan's work force, and as of 1978 over 70 percent
of these female employees were thirty years or older, and
two-thirds of them were married. This indicates that women
are no longer just office temporaries, earning money for their
wedding day. Most of these women will probably continue
to work in one capacity or another, and that will most likely
further alter the family situation.

One facet of family life in which the mother has played
a predominant role is education, where the *kyōiku mama* ("education mama") is a standard middle-class type pushing her
children to ever greater achievement in school and from one
battery of tests to another. The need to achieve is felt
strongly throughout Japanese society, and children in particular bear the brunt of the pressure to fulfill their parents'
wishes for them. Despite economic dependence on their husbands, however, Japanese women are quite emotionally independent, and this attitude is reflected in the popular phrase
"a good husband is healthy and absent," indicating a degree
of satisfaction with the traditional role of housewife and
mother that is inconceivable in other modern nations today.

In spite of occasional islands of independent activity, it is
for the most part not easy to encourage diversity in values
and life-styles in a country where over 100 million individuals speaking a common language and sharing a common culture are squeezed into four narrow islands. This basic setting

has affected the attitude toward work and workers' ability to preserve their privileges in the face of a world-wide economic slowdown. We have already noted how many observers have asserted that Japan's prosperity is fragile, and this argument has sometimes been used as a pretext to justify "rationalizing" employment in Japanese firms. The larger companies, however, do make a genuine effort to try every other solution before they finally resort to the layoff, which is the standard American corporate practice for cutting costs in a time of economic contraction. Transfers of personnel, extended vacations, pay cuts, and retraining of employees are all tried before mass firings are contemplated. If bad times continue for long, however, Japan may be faced with a labor crisis similar to that now threatening the rest of the industrialized world.

The Feminine Perspective in Japan Today
SUMIKO FURUYA IWAO

Let us imagine for a moment that half the population in the United States lives in the state of California and that we separate it from the rest of the United States, trim the edges and place it in the middle of the Pacific, put mountains onto 80 percent of the land, and have everybody inhabit the coastal areas. Then how would you expect people to behave? Competitive or noncompetitive? Individualistic or group-oriented? This imaginary island is in fact real—it is Japan, whose population is 120 million. The density of population in Tokyo is 5,300 persons per square kilometer, which means that people are living practically and literally on top of one another. The close proximity of others makes one sensitive to what others think, both about oneself and about everything else. On the positive side, crowding makes it necessary for the Japanese to be sensitive to others and to live in harmony, and the premium on space has also nurtured a very refined aesthetic taste. On the negative side, it has made the Japanese overly competitive and other-directed.

Japan is also a country of one ethnic group with one language, one skin color, and one class. Furthermore, the democratic ideal of equality has penetrated deeply into Japanese thinking, to the extent that over 90 percent of Japanese polled recently identified themselves as middle class. All these factors of homogeneity are conducive to easy comparisons with others and encourage the tendency to place everyone upon a unidimensional scale. In such a social environment, drastic attitudinal and behavioral changes rarely occur.

Since the end of World War II, women have been at least formally accepted as equals. Many institutions have been reformed so that women can now participate in politics and enjoy equal educational opportunities. In 1943 only 28 women in Japan graduated from universities. By 1950 there were 12,000 women graduates, and in 1975 the figure reached 250,000. Women now constitute 22 percent of students entering regular four-year universities and 88 percent of those entering junior colleges. This increase in the number of women in colleges is part of the reason the average age of marriage for women now stands at 24.9 years, two years later than in 1940. The average age of a woman when her youngest child begins school is now 34, whereas in 1940 it was 42. The average life span has also increased; it is now 77.9 years for women, 28 years longer than it was as recently as 1940. Not only has technology freed women from household drudgery, but better health and fewer children have bestowed upon them literally years more free time than the preceding generation enjoyed. The end of World War II proved to be the turning point in the improvement of women's legal and social position. However, institutional changes have not necessarily been accompanied by substantial changes in status. Let us first look at how women themselves have responded to the changes.

The question "Have you ever wished you belonged to the opposite sex?" always elicits an interesting response. The accompanying table shows the results of a 1953 survey conducted by the Institute of Statistical Mathematics in Tokyo, which indicated that a majority of Japanese females (64 percent) said they would have preferred to be born male. Only 27 percent were glad to have been born female. But in 1973, twenty years later, another survey found that the percentage

RELATIVE PREFERENCE TO BE BORN EITHER MALE OR FEMALE
(Percent Responding Affirmatively)

Year	Men		Women	
	Preference to be born male	Preference to be born female	Preference to be born male	Preference to be born female
	Japan[a]			
1953	94	2	64	27
1973	89	6	43	50
	United States[b]			
1959	96	4	17	83
1970	96	4	16	84

[a]Data from "Survey of National Character," Institute of Statistical Mathematics, Ministry of Education, Tokyo.
[b]Data from Gallup Poll.

of females who wished they could be born again as girls had increased to 50 percent. On the other hand, those who would have preferred to be male had dropped to 43 percent. In the United States, the Gallup Poll conducted a survey asking the same question in 1959 and again in 1970. In both years, 96 percent of American male respondents said they were happy to have been born males, while 83 percent of the women in 1959, and 84 percent in 1970, preferred to be females. In other words, the data obtained from American men and women on their gender preference remained quite stable. If we compare the Japanese data of 1973 with American and French data of 1970, the results are as follows: 90 percent of both French and Japanese men and 96 percent of American men are content to have been born males, while only 50 percent of Japanese women, 61 percent of French women, and 84 percent of American women are content with their gender. From these results one may surmise that even though Japanese women themselves are aware of their improved status, the lot of the Japanese woman—particularly compared to the American woman's—is still far from satisfactory. American, French, and Japanese men all overwhelmingly would prefer to be born again as males, which indicates that, as far as men are concerned, women are not in an enviable position, despite recent changes.

If we further analyze the data on Japanese women, it becomes evident that younger women would prefer to be reborn as females, while older women would rather be males. These findings seem to reflect the fact that the status of women in Japan has been improving over the years, though Japanese women do not enjoy as much status equality as Western women.

Another survey found that the most common reason 22 percent of Japanese women give for saying that they are glad to have been born female is that they can give birth and raise children. "Women have lots of fun" is the reason in 11 percent of the responses, and "Women do not have to work outside the home" is the reason given by another 11 percent. Among those who said that they are not happy as females, the most popular reason given is that their freedom is restricted. In any case, the results of this survey clearly show that motherhood is highly valued by Japanese women.

The next question that arises is how women react to having a job outside the home. The number of women entering the labor force in Japan has risen sharply in recent years; at present, women account for 37 percent of the total labor force. The number of married working women has also increased rapidly, though many are either part-time or temporary workers. In 1960 married women constituted about 25 percent of the female working force, but today they account for almost 65 percent. Young female workers today continue working an average of only 3.5 years for college graduates and 5 years for high school graduates, indicating that many stop working upon marriage. However, the accompanying graph shows that more and more women think it is desirable

IS IT "DESIRABLE" FOR WOMEN TO HAVE JOBS?
(Responses According to Ages of Women)

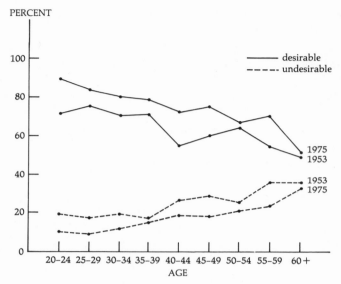

Source: "Survey of National Character," Institute of Statistical Mathematics, Ministry of Education, Tokyo.

to have a job. A survey conducted in 1977 by NHK, the Japan National Broadcasting Corporation, shows that 34 percent of married women think that women should give up their jobs while children are small and then go back to work once they are old enough to need less care, 27 percent think it is better to continue working if possible even after children are born, and 7 percent believe that women should not work at all. Of course, attitudes toward work do not necessarily coincide with actual behavior. Nearly 37 percent of the married women think that there is no discrepancy between their attitudes toward working and their present situations. Of those who claim that there is a discrepancy, 30 percent have given up doing anything about it and 14 percent feel they should do something but have done nothing, while less than 11 percent have taken some steps toward doing something, such as going back to school.

As already noted, Japanese women today have much more free time to devote to activities outside the home if they wish, yet the orientation is very strong toward remaining at home as a professional housewife. An NHK survey of women's attitudes asked a question many women may ask, "Do you find life in the home meaningful?" The overwhelming majority of women answered in the affirmative, with only 11 percent answering in the negative. The answers varied considerably, however, according to the respondent's age. The older the women, the greater the tendency to find home life worthwhile. It is evident that with other alternatives younger women do not enjoy home life as much as older women do.

Now let us look at women's roles in the family. The Japanese woman is usually thought of as submissive and subservient, but in the home she is the most powerful person. In the family the Japanese woman is the boss. The activities of the home revolve around her and depend upon her. In most cases, she controls the purse strings, and many husbands bring their salary envelope unopened to their wives. They are in turn given a monthly allowance. The housewife keeps the budget and manages the home. She is responsible for the physical and mental well-being of her husband and children. She is always available when her family needs her, and makes it a point to be home to greet children when they return from school. In the smooth running of the home, a woman can express her abilities. Asked whether they want their husbands to help around the house, 51 percent of housewives say they do, 39 percent do not want their help, and 10 percent have no opinion. One reason they may refuse the help of their husbands is that the home is their territory, and they want to keep it under their own control. In Japan, being a housewife does not carry the derogatory meaning that it may in the United States. Considering this tradition, it is not surprising that 49 percent of women say they agree with the idea that "the man's place is on the job; a woman's place is at home." Forty percent of women think otherwise. Therefore role separation not only exists but is supported by women themselves, albeit by a margin of only 9 percent. Many women do engage in such activities as part-time jobs, sports, consumer movements, and arts and crafts, but only as long as they do not interfere with the care of the family.

How do husbands respond to women in the home? Traditionally marriages were arranged "by the family, for the family," and wives were entirely subject to their husbands. Under the new 1947 Constitution, marriage is decided upon by the individuals concerned, and husband and wife officially have equal rights. Today the term "arranged marriage" usually means that the first meeting of the prospective couple has been arranged. If they decide they wish to get to know each other better after this meeting, they will continue to date; if their relationship grows closer they may fall in love and eventually marry. The person who initially introduces the couple usually takes into consideration such relevant factors as family and educational background, so that the two are well suited to each other. The likelihood that they will find each other compatible is therefore high, and the propensity to find a mate this traditional way increases with the female's age (see the accompanying graph). This pattern of meeting marriage partners is one reason the divorce rate is low in Japan. Once married, both husband and wife pursue their respectively expected roles; the husband becomes the breadwinner and the wife becomes the manager of the home. There is more emphasis on a complementary relationship between the couple than on sharing feelings and activities.

PROPORTION OF LOVE MARRIAGES TO
ARRANGED MARRIAGES AS OF 1972

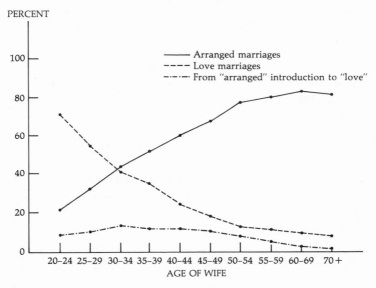

Source: "Survey of Attitudes about Women," Prime Minister's Office, Tokyo, 1973.

Marriage in Japan is like taking a tenured post, in the sense that both husband and wife have a tendency to take the relationship for granted. One survey found that 64 percent of women of various ages have never thought of divorce, 34 percent seldom think of it, and 2 percent are always thinking about it. There is an expression that children are the hinges that hold parents together, and the belief is firm that a broken family is detrimental to children. On the other hand, there is not much sanction against women who are divorced.

Communication between Japanese couples, except for newlyweds, may be minimal. One survey showed that married people talk to each other an average of thirty-eight minutes per day, and some wives converse with their husbands as little as six minutes per day. Traditionally love is seldom expressed verbally, but a strong sense of trust that exists between married people maintains their bond, although they do not know much about what the other is doing or receive frequent assurances of love. The role of Japanese wives as mother and manager of the home is far more important than their role as sex object or hostess. In urban society in particular, men typically turn to professional hostesses and conversationalists in geisha houses, fancy restaurants, or bars for satisfaction of needs not provided by, or indeed expected of, wives.

In short, a Japanese housewife lives quite independently of her husband and is thus emotionally very strong, although financially dependent on him. On the other hand, many Japanese men are helpless without their wives and therefore quite dependent. The common expression "A good husband is healthy and absent" accurately reflects the attitude of many Japanese women toward their husbands. An absent husband cannot interfere with his wife's activities, and the powerful Japanese housewife arranges her schedule and enjoys various kinds of activities as she wishes. Women usually dress up not for their husbands but to visit their women friends or to go shopping.

In contrast to the rather cool relationship a woman may have with her husband, she is very close to her children. Children are always the center of a mother's concern and the focus of emotional dependence. The fact that children are pivotal members of the family is reflected in the custom parents have of calling each other "Papa" or "Mama" even when children are not present or after they are fully grown.

Traditionally, great emphasis is placed upon learning and school education, and the literacy rate in Japan is 99 percent. There are nine years of compulsory education, and the percentage of college-age students entering college is 44 percent for boys and 34 percent for girls. The strong motivation to enter college is partly explained by the fact that a college degree from a good university is necessary for a young man to be employed by a reputable company and for a young woman to be able to marry a husband with good prospects. The university entrance examination is open to all, and its tremendous competitiveness is a major feature of the educational experience. Success or failure in entering a particular school is determined entirely by one's performance on the entrance examination. Under this system, parents who have established themselves among the elite strive to preserve that status by pressing their children to live up to their standards. Parents who wish to raise their status do everything they can to see that their children reach the goals the parents set for them. Children are thus forced into what can be quite vicious competition to pass the entrance examinations for prestigious universities. Before the end of World War II, when there were many children in each family, only one child (usually the eldest son) was duty bound to go along with the parents' wishes; the other children enjoyed more freedom. Now on the average there are only one or two children per family, and thus each child feels the pressure. Here the support of mothers is indispensable. Since there is so much emphasis on scholastic achievement, many mothers help their children with homework, provide moral support by bringing them snacks when they are working at home, and consider carefully which school to send them to. The greater the emotional and financial investment in the children's education, the greater a mother's desire to see her children accepted by an elite school. Naturally not all children are born with high scholastic aptitude, and when children are unable to fulfill parents' expectations, tragedy sometimes results. A mother's closeness to her children is usually maintained at least until they are married, and in the case of daughters often after marriage. Japanese children are not expected to be financially independent until they start working full-time or until they are married. In short, Japanese children are typically brought up in a very warm and stable family environment with a very close relationship to their mothers. When asked whom they admire most, many children, particularly boys, will say, "My mother." Children's attachment to their mothers is prolonged in Japan, and observations on university campuses show that much doodling and graffiti concern mothers. Because there is such pressure on children to pass school entrance examinations, they are often pampered and treated regally within the family. As long as they do well at school, they receive approval, and anything that might adversely affect children's scholastic achievement is avoided.

From the woman's point of view, as long as children consume their energy and demonstrate the potential to fulfill their dreams, there is great satisfaction in motherhood and home life. Difficulties begin when women realize that children have their own lives to live and may not necessarily live up to their parents' expectations. Japanese women often face the question "What is the real purpose of my life?" Even in cases where they have succeeded in putting children into the best schools, young people eventually leave home, and women must then find other things to do with their energy or to serve as emotional outlets. Some women find themselves left completely alone with retired husbands with whom they may suddenly realize they have nothing in common. They are too old to learn how to communicate with each other. Flower arranging, the tea ceremony, and poem-writing are all handy outlets for women, but the problem of learning what to do with the many remaining years after children become independent and husbands retire is a major problem for Japanese women today. I hope that it will not be long before Japanese women realize that they should not try to actualize themselves only through their children but should be emotionally independent of them.

Contemporary Japanese women are in search of a new identity not simply modeled after women in Western countries but built upon Japanese concepts of happiness and fulfillment. In Japan today, the trend is toward calm and objective research in exploring various options for women, and possibly for men as well.

The Aging and Affluent Nation
KAORU KOBAYASHI

One major concern of most Japanese people today is the rapid aging of the population. The Japanese enjoy improved health and public sanitation and better nutrition than ever before, even though they eat only one-twentieth the beef and one-third the dairy products American consumers do. They now exercise more and have all the good things and all the bad things of America. They are faddish and try to import everything Americans have. One example is the craze triggered by the translation of Dr. Spock's book on child care. While some of this contributes to the raising of Japanese longevity above U.S. levels, the Japanese also have the tremendous task of accommodating a greater number of aging people within the time span of only 45 years, whereas it took from 75 to 170 years for most Western countries to get adjusted to these demographic changes. From the beginning of the twentieth century until the end of World War II, the average life expectancy in Japan had been somewhere under 50 years. Now the average life expectancy is 73 years for males and 78 for females. The United Nations classifies countries with less than 4 percent of the population at 65 years or over as "young countries," and those having more than 7 percent in this age-bracket as "old countries." According to this definition, Japan became an "old country" in 1970. Although this quiet, invisible revolution did not arouse the Japanese public in general as keenly as the "Nixon shock" or the two "oil shocks," Japan is not yet ready—

either socially or institutionally—to meet these drastic changes.

In order to illustrate this point, let me describe something I personally found quite shocking to observe. This sad example is the growing popularity of visits by old Japanese people, mostly women, to a temple in Nara in the central part of Japan, commonly known as Pokkuri Temple. *Pokkuri* means a sudden, peaceful, quiet death without any distress. It is sad to watch hundreds of elderly people earnestly praying to Buddha for a peaceful, sudden death without suffering from any protracted illness, and placing undergarments on the altar to symbolize their desire not to undergo pain and anguish. Observing this, I was reminded of a news item I read in the *New York Times* during my exchange-student years in New York City in the late 1950s. It concerned the diary of an old woman who had died and whose body had not been discovered for almost two weeks. She wrote, "No visitors today. . . . Nobody called today. . . . No friend visited today."

As a young student brought up in a close-knit family atmosphere, I could not at that time feel the urgency of the problem of loneliness and alienation among the elderly, but this is now a Japanese problem as well. There have been accelerated efforts to cope with the changes brought about by increased longevity. For instance, the Japanese government recently urged all employers to extend the compulsory retirement age of 55 to 60 or more, and the Advisory Council on Social Security recommended that the government itself raise the coverage of national pension schemes and expand recipients' benefits. Nevertheless, since postwar cultures have been primarily youth-oriented, it is still at the sacrifice of the middle-aged and elderly that the shift to form a new social order can be achieved. Therefore we can anticipate painful social readjustments for some time to come. For instance, 80 percent of the current Japanese unemployed are between the ages of 55 and 64, whereas in the United States the percentage is lower.

This issue dovetails the one of insensitive treatment of workers referred to as *madogiwa zoku*. *Madogiwa* means "by the window," and *zoku* means a group or type of people. They are the middle-aged and older workers who are, in a manner of speaking, on the ledge of the company organization—are to be kicked out the window or laid off because the employers feel these workers can no longer be promoted in the company organization. On the more positive side, there are now so-called "silver and golden seminars," designed by the Mitsubishi Electric Enterprise Union to help assess problems of middle-aged and elderly union members and to help them redefine their life goals and career goals as well as cope with middle-age stress.

The Japanese have found themselves in a very awkward position all of a sudden, with everyone in the world telling them repeatedly that Japan is an economic superpower. Although Japan is an affluent country, enjoying one of the highest GNPs per capita in the free world, Japanese are perplexed because they do not feel all that affluent. This perception gap is very real, at least to the Japanese. Japanese homes are equipped with all kinds of electrical appliances. Last year almost four million Japanese traveled abroad and bought all sorts of luxury items and ate at the several hundred Japanese restaurants now existing in New York. There is no escaping these facts, but the Japanese cannot believe they are actually affluent.

A confidential report of the European Economic Community is said to have described Japan as "a nation of workaholics who live in what Westerners could regard as little more than rabbit hutches." Undoubtedly, many Japanese were furious at the racist undertone of this report, but I could sympathize with the Europeans' frustration, which apparently stems from Japan's substantial trade surplus with them. The harsh evaluation concerning rabbit hutches is quite valid: the so-called affluence of the Japanese is only skin-deep. It is a superficial, fragile prosperity. Japan still has comparatively poorly paved roads, the sewage system is still under-developed, and there is relatively little space for living and for public parks. Therefore, as far as the amenities of life and decent living conditions are concerned, Japan remains far behind "civilized" Western countries. It is in this area that Japan must work very hard to build a pleasant living environment and guarantee a stable livelihood through the establishment of a decent, meaningful social security system.

2

Japan:
The Search for Identity

Foreword

The Japanese spend more time and energy than perhaps any other people in trying to define what constitutes their peculiar national identity. That identity includes so many and diverse components that it is no wonder the Japanese themselves, not to mention foreigners, have such difficulty defining it. Richard Halloran, one of the panel discussants, described the present as a "second Heian period," a period of assimilation, adaptation, and rejection of cultural imports from the West. Many Japanese themselves feel that their "Americanization" after World War II drastically altered the nature of their society and especially the personality of the younger generation. It is true that young Japanese appear to be more self-involved, less dedicated, and somewhat more cynical than their parents, but the generational difference is not unique to Japan. In this part, panelist Yoshikazu Sakamoto goes so far as to state that many Japanese students have a much closer affinity with their counterparts in the United States than with their own parents. If that is true, then it serves to emphasize the way universal problems of modernization have influenced the Japanese sense of self-identity, and is not simply an example of Americanization. Nevertheless, Japanese often use the term "Americanization" to refer to the universal solvent of modernization, which certainly has affected the United States as much as it has any other country.

John Campbell, another discussant, emphasized that one's perception of one's nation is shaped very much by its contact with the outside world, and that the intensity of a person's national feeling is related to the degree one feels threatened by the outside world. This of course was clearly apparent in the wartime xenophobia in Japan, when the English language and baseball were banned, as were other "barbarian imports." But such extreme ethnocentrism, unleavened by curiosity and absorption of foreign ways and fashions, is truly rare for the Japanese in modern times. Indeed, panelist Nagayo Homma interpreted the wartime hysteria in Japan as nothing more than a "deviation" from the ongoing process he defined as the Americanization of Japanese culture. And yet Halloran and others have argued that the ability to search constantly to discover what is useful in other nations is part of the Japanese genius. In fact, Halloran went even further and said that, while pursuing these goals, Japan manages to be one of the few nations in the world today that goes about its business by minding its own business. Such introversion may reflect Japan's long self-imposed isolation under the Tokugawa regime or its great failure in the Pacific war or both. But the future remains an unknown quantity. Over the last century, the Japanese have expended much of their collective energy trying to catch up with the great powers. Now that they have done so, will the perception that they have lessons for the rest of the world become an important element in their own emerging identity?

Some conceptions or prejudices probably will not change, because the Japanese find it comfortable or convenient to maintain them. Such is the equation of modernization with "Americanization." Phrasing the argument in such terms makes it easier for the Japanese to distinguish between *gai* ("outside") and native elements, although it does complicate our understanding of the Japanese identity. Discussant John Campbell observed how that identity has changed over the years precisely because the way the Japanese view themselves has changed. So, for instance, before World War II, when Japan was intent on catching up to the Western powers militarily, the values that were touted as essentially Japanese included self-sacrifice, endurance, and suffering. The Japanese may still emphasize endurance *(gaman)* and perseverance *(gambaru)*, but these values seem to pale beside the search for comfort and pleasure in today's consumer-oriented culture. The very fact that energy conservation is viewed by modern-day Japanese as a necessary evil and not as a positive good that will strengthen the nation's moral fiber indicates how different from the past the emphasis is now, even when the same values are involved.

Homma called Tokyo a metaphor for modern Japan's search for identity, and so it is. Outlandishly modern and international on the one hand, no one would ever confuse Tokyo with any foreign metropolis. It rises like Atlantis, a city of unique smells, sounds, and sights. Yet upon first visiting a city like New York, the Japanese will snort, "Just like Tokyo." The Japanese themselves have lost some sense of what is unique about their own *modern* culture—and the Japanese have been modern long enough to have made a contribution in that sector. Yet they will probably persist for a little longer in equating Japanese culture with the past, and all things modern—like jazz and ice cream, to cite Homma's examples—with the United States.

Despite the extensive amount of borrowing, which has led to a feeling of being inundated by foreign cultures, the Japanese have, as Halloran pointed out, basically come to grips with themselves by themselves. Furthermore, since there appears to be no current model for Japan to follow, the point comes to mind that Japan may now have some lessons to teach as well as to learn, and in the future this may become a new self-confident element in the country's ever-changing yet remarkably stable conception of its identity.

Japan's Historical Quest for Identity
AKIRA IRIYE

I came to America a quarter of a century ago and have stud-
ied and worked primarily in the United States during the past
twenty-five years. Thus I may not represent a typical Japanese viewpoint, but I do feel I share a great deal with the
Japanese of my generation. This is the generation that went
to primary school during World War II and whose secondary
schooling came under the aegis of the American Occupation.
The transition from the fanatical and nationalistic wartime
education to the intentionally de-nationalizing postwar education has made a lasting impression on the members of this
generation. They still recall vividly how the history and ge-
ography that they had been taught until August 15, 1945,
were declared false overnight and how they were told to
substitute a new set of textbooks for the old, which until
then had embodied the truth. Such an experience showed
them how truth could be manipulated, how yesterday's vil-
lain could be today's savior, and how one's sense of identity
was itself subject to forces beyond one's control.

I thought of this experience when I was invited to address
the issue of Japan's search for identity. My generation is
perhaps an extreme example, but it is by no means excep-
tional in having experienced cataclysmic changes in a span
of but a few years. Perpetual and drastic change has characterized Japanese society since the middle of the nineteenth
century and has forced its people to look for ways to make
life meaningful. It has induced them to raise the question of

identity, not only for themselves as individuals but also for their country as a whole. Above all, it has led them to try from time to time to redefine the nation's position in, and relationship with, the world.

On the surface it might appear that, given the constant and often drastic changes in national life, the perceptions the Japanese have of themselves and of the world have undergone rapid transformation, with the result that there is no stability, no underlying unity in Japanese thinking. Yet it is possible to argue that despite this apparent confusion and uncertainty the search for identity has had a fairly coherent story. To illustrate this point, let me cite some opinion polls. In a survey conducted in 1970, respondents were asked what Japan should do to enhance its position in the world. The answers ranged from expanding economic strength to augmenting military power. But the bulk of the respondents chose continued economic development and social welfare rather than increased armament as the objectives they should strive for. In 1972 an opinion poll asked how Japan should best ensure its future security. The preferred answers were economic cooperation with all countries, active diplomatic negotiation, improvement of the people's livelihood, and promotion of cultural exchange with all other countries—not the use of military power. In 1973 more than 90 percent of over 4,200 interviewees said that they were proud of being Japanese, and 60 percent thought the Japanese people had some excellent qualities. At the same time, 70 percent believed they had a great deal to learn from foreign countries. In 1978, 2,400 Japanese were asked what the nation's international role should be in the near future. Eighty-two percent answered that Japan should promote cultural exchanges with other countries, and 71 percent thought that cooperation with other advanced countries to contribute to world prosperity was an important goal. Sixty-eight percent stressed assistance to underdeveloped countries, and only 23 percent answered that now that Japan had reached the status of a major economic power it should be willing to assert political leadership in the world.

These survey results are interesting because they point to certain themes in Japanese attitudes toward their place in the world. First, there is fascination with the question of power in world affairs. Second, there is a tremendous preoccupation with economic development and prosperity. And third, there is the frequent presence of the concept of culture when Japanese discuss international relations. I would like to review briefly each of these themes as they developed historically after the middle of the nineteenth century and to conclude with a few observations about the implications for the present.

There is nothing uniquely Japanese about the preoccupation with power, economic development, or culture. All countries are concerned with the maintenance of a level of force in order to survive, with more efficient and productive methods for providing for the material needs of the people, and with the preservation of cultural symbols to give meaning to their existence as nations. In the case of the Japanese, much of this preoccupation has been couched in terms of the country's relationship with the external world. From the moment that Perry's fleet appeared off the coast of Japan in the 1850s, the country's leaders came to understand that power was what mattered in relations among nations. From that time on, power—or what is called national strength—provided one comprehensive way of defining a national goal. The country had to become strong, acquiring guns and ships, and the people would have to be willing to work hard, pay high taxes, and contribute manpower for the armed forces. National politics would have to be reorganized to facilitate such efforts, and a sense of self-respect would be enhanced in proportion as the country increased its power.

In this sense Japan's search for identity was a simple task of trying to make the country one of the major world powers. When in 1905 victory was won over Russia, that search seemed to have been successfully concluded. Japan was now one of the great powers, in the company of Britain, France, the United States, and other mighty nations. Yet at the very moment of victory some Japanese began to wonder whether the successful augmentation of military power had really brought about national fulfillment. All the country had done, they pointed out, was endure hardship and shed blood so that the army and navy could inflict damage on other countries. The people's standard of living had not improved noticeably in the meantime. The country was still so backward economically that it had to borrow funds from abroad to administer the overseas territories acquired through war. The real strength of the nation, it was pointed out, lay not in the number of ships or divisions but in natural resources, in agricultural and industrial productivity, and in higher standards of living. Without such economic achievements Japan's vaunted might was an empty boast. The nation suddenly would not be able to compete with other advanced countries. Thus in a period of what the Japanese called "postwar management," after the war with Russia, they increasingly emphasized economic development, industrialization, and overseas trade as sources of national strength. In such a perspective Japan's national goal was defined primarily in economic terms. This view was no less nationalistic than the stress on military strength, and in some respects it was even more so in that the promotion of the people's well-being, industrialization, shipping, and other activities was designed to make the country richer and less dependent on foreign goods and capital.

By the end of World War I the initial stages of economic transformation had been reached, and Japan was emerging as a creditor nation with an increasingly urbanized and indus-

trializing economy. The strivings for military power and for
economic strength were frequently in conflict. The demands
of the army and the navy for further armament spending
were often resisted by those who thought such spending
would undermine efforts at investment in economic development at home. But the two objectives had some characteristics in common. One was that they both patterned
themselves after the advanced Western countries. In military
and economic spheres Japan was to transform itself so that
it would become as strong and as industrialized as the countries of Europe and America. Japan, in short, was to be Westernized. Second, in both conceptions it was assumed that
international affairs were characterized by competition, conflict, and uncertainty. The world was an arena for the struggle for power and for markets, and there were no such things
as trustworthy friends and stable customers. All nations
were in a potential state of war, whether militarily or
economically. In such a situation it was extremely difficult to
state how the nation should behave except to be realistic,
opportunistic, and pragmatic in trying to take advantage of
each shifting situation to maximize its security and interests.

For these reasons it is not surprising that the search for
identity did not stop with the effort to strengthen and enrich
the nation. Going beyond those objectives the Japanese won-
dered whether there would not have to be more durable and
more uniquely Japanese goals to serve as the country's defining characteristics. This was a difficult problem, for what was
more durable was not necessarily what was more uniquely
Japanese. In the years after World War I it was thought that
Japan was at last able to establish a sense of identity as a
nation committed to world peace, prosperity, and stability.
Instead of pursuing military strength and nationalistic
economic enrichment, the Japanese would couch their aspirations in terms of international cooperation and inter-

dependence, so that they would be able to contribute to world peace and understanding through their economic, political, and cultural activities. This was a prevailing sentiment during the 1920s, when the country's leadership self-consciously adopted a policy of disarmament, economic interdependence, and cooperation with the League of Nations and with other countries. Japanese identification with such an image would stress its position in the world as one of the partners in building a more peaceful, stable, and prosperous international society.

While this view was conducive to creating a sense of certainty about Japan's role in the world, it was vulnerable to criticism of being too Western-oriented. Such ideas as disarmament, interdependence, and cooperation were imports from Europe and America, and the vision of a cooperative international order was essentially confined to relations among the advanced industrial countries. The allegedly universal and durable values and principles were of Western origin, and in accepting them as applicable to themselves, the Japanese were trying to make themselves more like Westerners. This was the type of criticism leveled against the internationalists of the 1920s by those who thought Japan should stress its uniqueness instead of copying Western civilization. The nationalists regained their influence in the 1930s by undermining, through intimidation, assassination, and political maneuverings, the position of the Western-oriented leadership. They justified their assault on internationalism by arguing that internationalist principles had merely served to preserve Western dominance, and that for Japan to protect its interests it must be willing to act independently. It must establish a sense of national identity on other than Western-inspired foundations. It should recall its pre-nineteenth-century native tradition and dedicate itself to the eradication of Western influence from national life. It should also identify more closely with other Asians, and help them get rid of their Western masters. In such a perspective, the war against the United States and Great Britain was a war of national self-redefinition. It was, as wartime Japanese propaganda insistently pointed out, a cultural and ideological warfare as well as a struggle for physical survival.

This type of rhetoric sounded plausible as one alternative to the Western orientation of the earlier years. But in fact World War II demonstrated how bankrupt the new conception was. In the name of Asia's liberation from the West, the Japanese armed forces established control over other Asians. While the Japanese talked about Asia's cultural heritage, it was never clear just what that heritage consisted of and how it was related to the ruthless rule the army and navy were establishing throughout Asia. And those who tried to soften the impact of Japanese military rule by developing a vision of a new liberated Asia found it extremely difficult to go beyond such concepts as economic development, political stability, and cultural exchange among Asian countries, concepts that had been prevalent during the 1920s. In fact, in many wartime pronouncements designed to give the Japanese a sense of purpose and self-identity as they fought America and Britain, one finds mention of Japan's commitment to world peace, prosperity, brotherhood, and understanding. If these were the goals for which the Japanese were fighting, there would be little to distinguish their war aims and peace objectives from those of the United States and its allies. Although rhetorical similarities should not be confused with an identity of interests, the fact remains that the Japanese failed to substantiate the claim that they were fighting for cultural autonomy as well as for physical survival. They survived the war as a nation, but the establishment of a new cultural order had never gotten off the ground. Actually, it was precisely because of that failure that the postwar reaccommodation to Western values was accomplished with relative ease. Because the Japanese people had remained basically oriented toward Western civilization even while they tried to reject it, after 1945 it was not difficult to redefine Japanese identity in terms of Western ideas and concepts.

The difference between prewar and postwar Japan was that after the war military power was discredited and never did provide a symbol of national purpose and commitment. Instead, economic activities and cultural pursuits became national preoccupations. In a sense the nation was going back to the priorities and concerns of the 1920s, when it attempted to identify itself with what appeared to be worldwide movements toward economic integration and cultural interchange. Those Japanese who considered these activities to be Japan's main contribution to peace and its principal means of safeguarding security were echoing the sentiment of the older generation who had experienced the internationalism of the 1920s. People of the generation born after 1930 did not, of course, experience the decade of the 1920s, but they too share an image of the twenties as a brief period of peace and liberalism before the country plunged into disastrous and fanatical warfare. If one has a negative image of the 1930s and 1940s, one would have to go back to the 1920s as a point of departure for a more acceptable pattern of national existence. There are those in Japan today who wonder whether —just as the short-lived internationalism of the 1920s gave way to the militarism, nationalism, and power politics of the next decade—history might not repeat itself, whether there might not be developing domestic and international trends that could provoke the resurgence of militant and anti-Western nationalism. Certainly there seems to be much less resistance today to public discussion of Japan's military and security position in Asia. Many observers have openly called for reevaluation of the country's defense policy and strategic planning, in view of the apparent passing of U.S. military supremacy in Asia, the Sino-American rapprochement, and the growing strength of the Soviet Union. These developments compel a reappraisal of the question of power, and the Japanese are once again being teased with the prospect of playing a power-oriented role in changing Asia. Economically, too, nationalistic sentiment has been fostered by trade disputes with the United States and with the European community, and by the failure of the advanced industrial countries to achieve more solid cooperation to cope with urgent energy and environmental problems. Economic internationalism has lost some of its appeal in an era of controlled growth and in a world where developing countries are asserting their nationalistic priorities, no longer satisfied with being part of an economic order defined by the rich nations.

In the realm of culture, there has been in Japan a growing interest in non-Western countries. Today's Japanese generally seem to have few illusions about Russia, unlike Japanese of the prewar years, who at times viewed Soviet socialism as a viable alternative. China's attractiveness, too, has begun to be questioned by some people, because of its foreign policy that often belies its profession of antihegemonism. Under these circumstances, more and more Japanese have been drawn to countries such as Mexico and India as inspiration for alternatives to customarily accepted values. Instead of posing the dichotomy of West versus East, some observers have argued that Japan must identify not with the rich and powerful West or with the parochial East but with the multiplicity of small and medium-sized countries that make up the bulk of the world.

Whether these trends will in time create a new orientation for Japan remains to be seen. I would merely observe, in conclusion, that it would be extremely unfortunate both for Japan and for other countries if economic and cultural internationalism were once again discarded as unworthy goals, and if military power came to be the only preoccupation of the Japanese people. I hope they will continue to resist the temptation of excessive arms buildup and power politics and to reaffirm their commitment to internationalism. I am somewhat confident that they will do so, because opinion polls consistently indicate general acceptance of the postwar emphasis on internationalism, and those polls indicate that this internationalist orientation has deeper prewar roots and is part of the modern Japanese legacy. It may be in need of some redefinition, given the growing influence of countries that do not share the precepts of Western-inspired internationalism. Still, I see no reason why the process of redefinition should involve the abandonment of a commitment to cultural openness, intellectual freedom, and economic interchange. Modern Japan has benefited tremendously from a world environment that has cherished these objectives, and it can now give something in return. Japan needs an interdependent community of nations, but instead of being merely a passive receiver of the benefits of such a community, it can contribute to the preservation and improvement of the community. It may be that the well-known proclivity of the Japanese people to stress harmony and avoidance of conflict in interpersonal relations, and their tendency to seek security in a dependency relationship, may yet prove to be assets in a world still dominated by power politics and egoistic nationalisms. Instead of trying to identify with such tendencies, Japan should, in its search for identity and meaning, ask how best to make use of the nation's deeply ingrained traits to make a contribution, however modest, to creating a more open world.

Frameworks of Japanese Identity
YOSHIKAZU SAKAMOTO

Since the 1860s, when Japan brought its long seclusion to an end and began to be incorporated into the Western state system, Japan has defined its identity in terms of the Orient versus the Occident. This dichotomy refers to two factors that were considered by the Japanese to be of fundamental importance. One is the cultural distinction between the East and the West, and the other is the gap between the two in terms of economic development and development of science and technology, including military technology. There was an element of ambivalence in Japan's response to this situation. Concerning the first factor, Japan stressed the need for preserving its cultural identity and spiritual authenticity. This represented a rejection of Western civilization. Concerning the second factor, however, Japan endeavored to catch up, namely, to identify itself with the West, which led to a dilution, if not a denial, of its identity. The net result of this ambivalent and complex development was the emergence of Japanese militarism—i.e., the traditional warrior's culture armed with modern technology—which finally led to the Pacific war.

Since the cultural and moral value system in prewar Japan was so tightly geared to militarism, the military defeat in 1945 naturally created a tremendous moral vacuum, which gave rise to a disintegration of national identity. Through the Occupation, which was virtually under the sole administration of the United States, and through the subsequent intensification of the Cold War, Japan entered a second phase, when it began to define its identity in terms of "the East versus the West" in a new context. Japan's new identification with the West differed from the previous form of Westernization in that the postwar Westernization was initiated parallel to (and even as a means to) the demilitarization of Japan.

Japan's new identification with the West was to be nonmilitary in two respects. First, unlike the prewar Westernization, the postwar Westernization called for modernization of Japan's political system on the Western model. However, the postwar Westernization, in the context of increasingly intense East-West conflict, brought external pressures to bear on Japan to rearm itself. Had Japan done so at the pace and on the scale urged by the United States at the height of the Cold War in the 1950s, it is all too likely that Japan would have been remilitarized even to the extent of being taken over by the military. In this connection it may be noted that successful military coups in the postwar period were not the monopoly of the Third World, but could be observed also in Westernized countries, such as Greece. Under the circumstances, the Japanese faced a dilemma: they had to avoid Japan's full-fledged military commitment to the West precisely in order to reinforce the reform of the domestic political system on a Western model.

Second, the postwar demilitarization of Japan gave rise to a tendency among the Japanese to equate the nonmilitary approach with an economic approach, and peace with economic development—hence the tendency to regard economic growth at home as a pure good, and economic expansion abroad as a nonmilitary and thus peace-oriented and therefore irreproachable enterprise. The fallacies and dilemmas inherent in this approach came to the fore in the early 1970s, when environmental disruptions became intolerable and the OPEC strategy revealed the fragile base of the Japanese economy in terms of resource supply. It was in response to the impact of the OPEC embargo in 1973, and the anti-Japanese protest movement in Southeast Asia which confronted the Japanese prime minister on his visit to that region in 1974, that Japan belatedly began to define its identity in terms of the North versus the South, in addition to the East-West dichotomy.

In the context of North-South conflict, Japan again found itself faced with a dilemma. Since the 1860s, Japan has been almost totally preoccupied with how to catch up to the more advanced countries in Europe and North America. In 1973 Japan was for the first time forced to recognize seriously the fact that there are many peoples in the South who are desperately trying to catch up to the North, including Japan. And in this respect Japan itself is being pursued by the late-comers. While Japan will continue to try to keep pace with the United States and Western Europe, especially in terms of per capita income and the quality of life, it has come to realize that it must also transform and adjust itself with a minimum of tension and conflict to meet the legitimate needs of developing countries.

All that I have said so far indicates that Japan's definition of its national identity has always contained a considerable degree of ambivalence, which in the final analysis stems from its relatively peripheral position within each of the three frameworks mentioned. In terms of the Orient-Occident dichotomy, Japan, being the most Westernized Asian nation, is on the fringe of both the Orient and the Occident. In terms of East-West conflict, Japan again is on the fringe of the West —not only because of its geographical proximity to the Soviet Union and China, but also because of the immaturity of its democratic institutions as represented by the continuing dominance of one party on the national level. In terms of North-South conflict, Japan again is located on the fringe of the North not only in terms of per capita income as distinct from GNP, but also for (1) the lack of stable regional partners, unlike the countries of the European community, and (2) the lack of a high degree of self-sufficiency in resource supply as compared with the United States. These peripheral characteristics of Japan's international position have contributed to creating special difficulties for the Japanese in establishing an unambiguous image of their national identity.

In addition to these obstacles on the international level, however, there seem to be more fundamental changes taking place within Japanese society which have precipitated the identity crisis. These changes are taking place in Japan because the country has begun to move into the so-called postindustrial stage; therefore they are not unique to Japan but are shared by other highly developed societies. I refer to the erosion of the fundamental cultural frameworks that have laid the groundwork for the definition of identity in the long history of humankind. Let me illustrate four facets of the problem. First, from time immemorial human society has consisted of male culture and female culture. The distinction between the two was self-evident in most societies. Today it has become increasingly difficult to distinguish clearly between what is culturally (as opposed to biologically) unique to the male and what is culturally unique to the female. Second, from primitive societies to modern society a clear distinction could be observed between the adult culture and nonadult youth culture. Ceremonies to register the initiation of the nonadult were very common in many premodern societies. In modernized societies commencement at the end of college education or service in the army performed a similar function. Today the youth begins to know and live an adult life at a much earlier stage of personal growth than in the past, whereas the adult exposed to rapid social change and subject to the need for continuing lifelong education and self-education tends to be less confident that today's adult culture will be that of tomorrow. Third, the line distinguishing between elite culture and mass culture is also being blurred. In the past the elite were clothed differently, spoke differently, ate differently, and were educated differently from the masses. It was not difficult to perceive at a glance who belonged to the elite and who did not. Today it has become increasingly difficult to tell cultural distinctions between the elite and the masses. Of course, the distinction in terms of the allocation of power still exists between the elite and the masses, but culturally the elite are no longer in a clearly higher position, which partly explains the decline of the authority and reverence that used to characterize political power when it was more or less accepted by the ruled. Finally, the distinction between national cultures is becoming more difficult to maintain, due to the increasing interpenetration of cultures across national boundaries. This of course does not mean that cultural diversity will disappear, but it does mean that national boundaries will increasingly lose their importance as a line of demarcation of different cultures. For instance, many of my students have a much closer sense of cultural affinity with their counterparts in the United States than with their parents. They and their parents speak the same Japanese, but they do not have a common language, whereas they and the youth in America have a common language, although they speak different tongues. In this respect, for many of my students their parents are the foreigners, and their generational counterparts in the United States are the compatriots. A similar process is also taking place in many of the Western European countries.

Obviously, these changes in the basic cultural structure can be observed primarily in the developed societies, and what I have said does not apply to most of the societies now developing, but they too are likely to be subject to similar change in the future. All in all, the erosion of the fundamental cultural framework undoubtedly contributes to deepening the crisis of identity that the Japanese are undergoing. How then can we establish a clear image of Japanese national identity in the context of a rapidly changing world? In the light of the fundamental changes in cultural structure which are taking place beyond national boundaries, it would probably be a mistake to try to identify distinctively national attributes in order to reformulate and redefine Japan's identity. What we should do is identify those unique characteristics of Japanese society that simultaneously have international or even global implications. Along this line of thinking, I draw your attention to four characteristics unique to Japanese society that have much broader implications for the world as a whole.

First, Japan is the only nation in the world that has actually experienced a nuclear war. The Japanese know from Hiroshima and Nagasaki what World War III would be like in concrete human terms. Memory of the atomic holocaust is still vivid, especially in the mind of older generations, while the youth are more sensitive to the hazards involved in the industrial use of nuclear energy. The uniquely strong reactions of the Japanese in this respect are being called by some people a "nuclear allergy," but for me and for most of the Japanese, that kind of allergy is a sign of health. From the nuclear experience we can draw a policy recommendation that Japan should establish its identity by assuming a more active and positive role in the area of disarmament, especially nuclear disarmament on a global scale.

Second, it has long been recognized that Japan is the only country in the non-European world that has attained a high degree of economic development, much ahead of many non-European nations. Today everybody knows that the cult of economic growth that prevailed in Japan in the 1960s was a mistake, but it is also a mistake to dismiss Japan's economic achievement in terms of upgrading the level of well-being of the masses. What then should Japan do in light of this experience? It is evident that Japan should establish its identity by promoting more actively its cooperation with the Third World nations, not only in the form of extending more aid, as have the United States and Western European countries, but also in the form of critically sharing Japan's historical experience, especially with respect to Japan's success in the *selective* introduction and assimilation of foreign technology that meets local needs.

Third, Japan was and to some extent still is a most "advanced" country in terms of environmental deterioration. Thanks to the pressure of public opinion, the Japanese government—national and local—as well as the judiciary, took measures to redress grievances. But these measures came too late for the victims of horrifying pollution, as illustrated by Minamata, a village which suffered wholesale tragedy as a result of the mercury-contaminated waters from which its fishermen had always derived their livelihood. Instead of trying to mitigate ecological pressures at home by exporting pollution-emitting industries abroad, especially to developing countries, Japan should give warning to the world by disseminating information on its bitter experience and on the measures it has taken to prevent environmental deterioration. Japan should also take every step to build a pollution-free society as a model for other countries, especially for the developing countries.

Fourth, Japan is one of the poorest countries in the world as far as resource supply self-sufficiency is concerned. Of course there are poorer countries in terms of the absolute amount of locally available resources, but when it comes to the ratio of locally available resources to the amount of resources required to sustain the present standard of living, Japan undoubtedly falls under the category of the resource-poorest. Accordingly, Japan should make every effort to (1) develop highly resource-saving technology, especially alternative technology for energy utilization, and (2) modify and change the value priorities of society as well as the individual's life-style, in order to create a model of a highly resource-saving society.

If Japan succeeds in building a society that is nuclear-free, pollution-free, oriented to global equity, and resource-saving, it will have significant implications beyond establishing Japan's national identity, because all four of the characteristics mentioned have a direct bearing on world constraints as a whole. Not only Japan but also the entire globe is subject to the threat of nuclear war and faced with the need to eliminate poverty, to prevent environmental disruptions, and to survive in a decent, humane way despite limited resource supply. These are the major problems confronting humankind as a whole. Therefore, if Japan succeeds in solving those problems that seem to be unique to it, its experience will have tremendous implications for the future of the world as well.

3

Japanese Culture: Continuity and Change

Foreword

Part 2 was concerned with Japan's attempt to define its identity in the face of wholesale infusions of foreign cultures. Yet one must admit, as panelist Shuji Takashina pointed out, that many features of Japan's cultural heritage which are usually thought of as uniquely Japanese, such as the tea ceremony, Zen, and so on, were once imported from abroad. There is a delightful irony in this, since the Japanese have so often been dismissed as imitators and yet in certain respects the very things they did copy have come to be admired as representing distinctive artifacts of Japanese culture!

What then is Japanese culture? One thing is for certain: Japanese culture is no more immutable than the culture of any other society. Panelist Masakazu Yamazaki argues in this part that Japan's cultural landscape changed profoundly as a result of the national seclusion and rigid class system established by the Tokugawa shogunate. Originally a sociable and outgoing people, after the sixteenth century the Japanese became reserved, almost timid, in social intercourse. The vibrancy of the preceding Muromachi period (1336–1573) may only now be reentering Japanese life as a consequence of the country's increasing interdependence with the rest of the world. Most people today would be amazed to hear that the Japanese were actually rather swashbuckling before the Tokugawa, and that their pirates and traders were known and feared throughout East Asia. History sometimes repeats itself.

Perhaps such seeming repetition really amounts to what Takashina called a culture of integration and coexistence rather than one of succession and rejection. This implies that the Japanese never reject what is old, even as they eagerly embrace the new and the fashionable. It also helps to explain why certain foreign imports have managed to acquire a "made in Japan" label over the centuries. *Gagaku,* ancient court music, is just one example of an art that disappeared long ago in its land of origin (China), while it is still very much alive in Japan, where performances may be heard every year.

When discussing culture, one inevitably enters the misleading terrain of stereotypes, those propagated by natives as well as by foreigners. One favorite stereotype cherished by both groups is the alleged Japanese love of nature, embracing as it does a desire to cooperate and closely interact with nature—to respect it—rather than to conquer or dominate it. Discussant Donald Keene took issue with this popular conception, countering that in a sense the Japanese almost hated nature. Think of *bonsai:* what more dramatic form of dominating nature can there be, he asked. Nature in a garden is preferred to nature in the raw—nature as modified by human preference rather than the original article. In fact, the Japanese appreciation of nature is a complex matter, used often more as a convention, as in poetry and art, than as a real, heartfelt love. The great *haiku* poet Bashō, in fact, wrote very little about nature and spent most of his words on man. Similarly, the predominant element in *The Tale of Genji* scroll is human beings, not nature.

Keene likewise countered the opinion which emphasizes continuity in Japanese culture when he recollected that a mere twenty years ago most Japanese were certain that there were very distinct, sharp breaks in Japan's cultural history, the greatest ones being the Meiji Restoration of 1868 and

Japan's defeat in 1945. As with all such matters, one's perspective is critical in determining one's conclusion. In this part Kazuko Tsurumi brings her unique perspective to the feature of homogeneity so often treated as a given of Japan's culture. In taking issue with this view, she cites the area of religious belief, which in Japan is highly eclectic. This is almost like having the inhabitants of Maruyama's "octopus pots" (see p. 12) sample from many different "pots" without losing their own identity. The penchant for sampling and the notorious receptivity of the Japanese in this area, as well as in the arts, demonstrate once again their uncanny capacity for "Japanizing" whatever they choose to adopt.

Social Intercourse in Japanese Society
MASAKAZU YAMAZAKI

For over a decade the Japanese have been gradually exposed
to the international community and have often been criti-
cized for their poor sociability. Many foreigners, both those
living in Japan and those living abroad, point out unani-
mously that Japanese are too shy on social occasions and that
their public speeches, especially those of politicians and
businessmen, seldom show a sense of humor. Japanese who
have lived abroad for a while also complain about the scarcity of opportunities in Japan to be invited to private
gatherings like home parties, and make no secret of their
disappointment at the lack of public places for socializing
such as theaters, concerts, or cabarets. Unfortunately, both
these criticisms are correct. It is true that the Japanese have
been indifferent about the concept of sociability, if not
actually unsociable. Most recently they have been little interested in the art of social intercourse, the style and the
technique of communicating and entertaining one another.
Japanese have not much consciousness of playing a lively
role and directing one's actions as an actor on the stage of
interpersonal relationships. Over the years since the Edo
period in the seventeenth century, modesty has been the
only virtue accepted among women, and among men reti-
cence has received more respect than eloquence. And those
who keep criticizing this tradition in the postwar period as
a remnant of the so-called feudalistic mentality have merely
tried to introduce intimacy and frankness into the communi-

cation process and never think of the importance of the art and style of self-expression. Today, both at home and at school, training in social manners is not emphasized as much as intellectual education, and training in spoken Japanese is practically neglected. When an art of any kind declines, it is always threatened from two opposing directions, namely, extreme formality and excessive naturalism. This applies to the Japanese culture of human relations too.

Social gatherings in the Japanese community are sharply divided into two categories: the most formal and the purely informal. On formal occasions, like wedding banquets or official ceremonies, everything is so stiff and ritualistic that the spontaneous exchange of human feelings is completely hampered. In informal gatherings, people are absorbed in sheer merrymaking and forget all their manners. This dichotomy is also recognized in the actions of individuals in their daily lives. People spend their daytime hours in public places like the office, where they confront others in stereotyped roles, assuming mannered postures and speaking with conventionalized politeness. On the other hand, people spend their nights in the purely private world, where they rest at ease, maintaining a totally relaxed attitude, taking almost no trouble to be hospitable to others. And between these two extremes of public life and private life (the daytime and nighttime attitudes), there is almost no intermediate dimension to Japanese life. In fact, this dichotomy is a vital menace to the idea of sociability, because the art of social intercourse, not unlike that of the theater, consists of something in between the formal and the informal, between intensity and relaxation. It takes a sort of delicate mixture of the theatrical and the carefree attitude to make a social blend. Like actors, people are supposed to be constantly conscious about every gesture and word with which they express themselves and yet look perfectly natural to others. Again, metaphorically,

contemporary Japanese are not theatrical enough to be genu-
inely sociable, because they are either excessively stylistic or
overnaturalistic.

Perhaps related to this phenomenon is the fact that the
theater is much less popular than any other major cultural
activity in Japan. I do not mean that the Japanese theater
itself is dull or inactive in terms of artistic creativity, but it
is far from thriving. There is a striking contrast between the
enormous amount of advertising for books and the meager
column for theater appearing in the daily newspaper. There
is no quarter comparable to the West End or Broadway in
Tokyo, a city that can well compete with London or New
York in the other areas of culture such as publishing, broadcasting, and education. It must be noticed that the theater not
only offers a place for sociality in its foyer but also supplies
illustrative lessons for self-expression from its stage. And
those on stage can coach the audience in how to speak their
language beautifully, and be models for how to behave in
situations one may encounter in this world. From this point
of view, too, Japanese today—particularly the young—are
suffering from the absence of one of the most effective classrooms for social intercourse.

However, a particular phase in the history of a nation does
not necessarily reveal the essential face of the nation's character. Sometimes the culture of a nation can be accidentally
distorted when one focuses on a limited period of time, and
such is the case with Japan.

Ironically, social intercourse was originally one of the
foundations of Japanese culture. The traditional art genres
like the tea ceremony, flower arrangement, and linked verse
obviously originated and flourished as entertainment for the
social gatherings that medieval Japanese were so enthusiastic
about. It may be safely said that classical poetry as a whole
was a product of the sociability of the court nobles. Most of

the classic poems, both *tanka* and *haiku,* were actually composed right in the middle of poetry parties and then recited by their authors and critiqued by the other participants. In the sense that the poets principally created their work in front of an audience, Japanese classic poetry may be considered a kind of performing art. Even the fine art of the sixteenth century had a kind of histrionic sensibility. Also, the theater itself was no doubt the most flourishing and representative art form of medieval Japan. The political rulers of the sixteenth century patronized Nō and Kyōgen and made them the official entertainment for their courts. Thus the theater was fully authorized as a legitimate part of public culture and able to attract its audience from all classes of the society. In fact, the social status of the Japanese theater was not unlike that in the West, inasmuch as the theater of the West also thrived under the protection of the state, and was recognized as an indispensable part of the public culture. Furthermore, the general character of the people of sixteenth-century Japan seems to have been much different from that of their modern descendants. They were ardent party-goers, sophisticated hosts, eloquent discussants, and even internationally open-minded. Hideyoshi, the famous military ruler of the sixteenth century, hosted an enormous open-air tea party in 1587, to which he invited all kinds of people from the emperor down to commoners, and even foreigners. A Jesuit missionary, Francis Xavier, testified that the Japanese of his time were far from being shy and that they visited him so often to ask questions that he could hardly get any sleep. Another missionary, Organtino, reported that the two vices Japanese hated most were an impatient attitude toward other people and irrationality in discussion. According to the report that the missionary wrote home, the questions asked by the local people of Kyūshū seemed to have been of quite sophisticated, philosophical substance, even judged by present standards. For example, in response to the doctrine that Christianity is universal and eternal truth, they asked, "Why, then, has it not been propagated prior to this particular time in history?" If Christianity were indeed the eternal teaching, they claimed, Japanese should have known about it from the beginning of history. The missionaries were greatly troubled by the logical arguments of the Japanese of the time, and Xavier confessed that he finally came to fear that he was being subjected to a kind of religious persecution.

In view of the striking change in the character of the Japanese national culture, one cannot help but assume that something happened between the mid-seventeenth century and today which twisted the course of Japan's cultural development. It is all too well recognized that the seventeenth-century Tokugawa (Edo) shogunate followed an isolationist policy that alone must have changed the national character to a considerable degree. But this was not by any means all that happened during the Edo period. What was most significant for cultural history was that the austere and moralistic regime despised and discouraged social intercourse. In sharp contrast to preceding shogunates, the Tokugawa regime stopped giving public support to all cultural activities, expelling them into a narrow, private world and severing their relationship with politics. Only school education and moralistic readings were excepted. Among the performing arts, Nō drama was the only exception given shogunate approval, but it too was institutionalized, as a ceremonial art of the rulers, and its ties with the people were broken permanently. On the other hand, the leading arts from other periods, such as *kabuki, ukiyoe,* the love novels, and most of the musical works, were all exiled from public places and confined to the world of the pleasure quarters. It is true that with the rich economic support of the townspeople this confined world itself became full of vitality and nourished cultural activities. But it is undeniable too that most of the Japanese arts lost the legitimacy openly confirmed by a healthy society. Their forms and styles were also distorted to a considerable degree.

What was most decisive for Edo culture was that the nature of banquets, which were central to social life, underwent a substantial change. The Western-style banquet, conducted in a huge open space under sparkling chandeliers, is a mechanism for seeking an intimate human relation while maintaining distance and tension. Such formalities as a table speech, in which one can show off one's eloquence, and the toasts and ballroom dancing executed with a theatrical touch are conceived with this idea in mind, and together with other similar circumstances the banquets of this style no doubt provided a proper environment for Western art to develop sturdy and large-scale compositions. Banquets in Japan had a similar characteristic in the sixteenth century, but in the Edo period they lost their public quality and were confined to small rooms in the pleasure quarters, like geisha houses, where dim light from lanterns instead of chandeliers flickered, where personal exchanges of sake cups rather than toasts were made, where intimate singing in a low voice rather than eloquent speeches or ballroom music was heard. In such a milieu, there was no need to maintain distance and tension, nor was there any need for exploratory effort to build a private relationship. It is not difficult to imagine that such a change in the manner of social intercourse had a significant effect on the behavior of the Japanese and their art forms as well, which are delicate and subtle but all too fragile.

Unfortunately, modernization in the Meiji era (1868–1912) began to move in a direction that aggravated rather than rectified this cultural distortion created by the times. Modernization gave the government more centralized power than that of the Edo regime, and a strong impetus to follow the national policy was present in the movement of private capital as well. As a result, the whole investment of the nation concentrated on the so-called "official culture," namely, school education and reading, which had been approved since the Edo period. Thanks to this cultural monomania, modern Japan can boast the world's highest literacy rate and a flourishing publishing industry. In contrast, plays, music, and fine arts have remained in an unusually poor environment. Plans for national theaters and concert halls did not materialize until after World War II, and the concept of public support for artists has yet to take firm root. Moreover, even formal education has not provided a place for training in emotional expression. The conservative teachers of manners of the prewar time urged students not to express any free emotion, and self-styled progressive teachers of the postwar period are encouraging students to reveal their true sentiment without teaching them how to express it properly. Consequently, most modern Japanese have been suffering from the accumulation of amorphous and nameless feelings, which are to be exposed only through a sulky silence or an inscrutable smile. It should be emphasized that these ambiguous feelings such as shyness and embarrassment are by no means an essential characteristic of Japanese psychology but are the malady of an epoch by which Japanese continue to be tortured.

There is every indication that many Japanese have begun using their leisure time for social occasions rather than for reading books or watching TV at home. So-called "service businesses" like restaurants, cafeterias, hotels, and travel agents are increasingly thriving, in spite of the rather stagnant condition of the Japanese economy. One may be surprised to see luxurious restaurants and hotel lounges in Tokyo full of housewives and elderly people chattering over lunch or coffee during the daytime. Most indicative, however, is the skyrocketing number of people attending lifetime education classes provided by both private and public institutions. The Asahi Cultural Center, for example, managed by the Asahi newspaper company, by itself attracts more than 20,000 registered students every year, and there are hundreds of similar institutions in Tokyo now. In the city of Toyama, a typical regional city of about 300,000, more than a thousand adults formed a queue to enroll as members of the "Citizens' University." It may appear that the education-oriented Japanese are once again showing their unchangeable nature. But what these classrooms are offering them is in fact an ideal occasion to get together and speak to one another, and to use the admirable pretext of education for doing so. There they can enjoy discussing *The Tale of Genji* or *A Midsummer Night's Dream* with their tutors and fellow students, and after a while they move over to a nearby coffeehouse to continue their pleasant conversations. All kinds of sports, which are also becoming popular at an amazing pace these days, function in exactly the same manner. Tennis clubs and jogging groups provide citizens with places where they can meet others from distant areas and different age-brackets. They learn how to adjust to strangers and how to compete with one another in a more sophisticated manner.

Such indications of change in the life pattern of the Japanese have already been noticed by various sectors of the society. A book entitled *The Cultural Industry,* written by a banker, portrays the future of the mobile society and was ranked among the best-sellers of the year. The late Prime Minister Ōhira, in his inaugural speech to the Diet, remarked that Japan was finally entering the age of culture after passing through the ages of politics and economy of the postwar period. I personally hope that this prophecy will come to pass and that Japan in the future will not only recover from the postwar confusion but also rectify its centuries-long cultural distortion.

Cultural Heterogeneity and Japanese Shinto
KAZUKO TSURUMI

A discussion of religious beliefs centering on State Shintoism versus Folk Shintoism might sound esoteric, but two recent events reveal that this is still a very lively issue. The first is the recent disclosure that fourteen class-A war criminals, including wartime prime minister and ex-general Tōjō, executed by the International War Tribunal, were secretly enshrined in 1978 in the Yasukuni Shrine as "martyrs of the Showa period." Shortly after the disclosure, the late Prime Minister Ōhira paid homage as "a private person" to the shrine on the occasion of its annual spring festival. It is important to note that the enshrinement of the wartime leaders was covert, without publicity, which is an indication that those who were responsible for the action were afraid of public criticism.

Second, the bill to institutionalize the Imperial era name based on the specific emperor's reign was initiated by the government and pressed hard in the Diet, where it was finally passed on June 6, 1979. The government explained that this was necessary to guarantee the continuation of the Imperial era name after the present Emperor. According to public-opinion polls, the majority of the people said that they were using the Imperial era as a custom and that they preferred to use it as such, but not as a compulsory practice. The government, however, utilized the results of the polls to claim that people supported the legal enforcement of its usage. The bill having passed, it is now feared that it might result in emphasizing the Emperor's position beyond that of "the symbol of national unity," as defined in the present Constitution. Critical views are being voiced not only in editorials but also in letters to editors in various newspapers by people of different walks of life.

These current events reveal that State Shintoism is on the wane but not exactly dead. In order to understand these current issues, a brief look at the historical context may be helpful. Japanese culture is not homogeneous, as stereotyped notion tells us, but consists of heterogeneous cultures brought by heterogeneous peoples from the time of the Jōmon period, beginning in 8000 B.C., to the Tomb period, ending in the fourth century A.D. At least five immigration routes are identified: (1) from Siberia, (2) from the Korean peninsula, (3) from East China, (4) from South China, and (5) from the islands of Southeast Asia. The Japanese islands are where the people from the North and from the South met, and beliefs and rituals that came with the newcomers were homogenized at a relatively early stage. Mixing of beliefs, native and foreign, has been the characteristic trait of Japanese religion and culture from the very beginning.

Japanese native religious beliefs are called Shintoism. Under this name, at least six different varieties of beliefs are classified: first, Primitive Shintoism, a combination of animism, worship of nature and spirits of the dead, and two kinds of Shamanism, that of the Northern Tungus fused with the shamanistic rituals associated with rice cultivation in Southeast Asia. Second, from the seedbed of Primitive Shintoism, Shrine Shintoism flowered—simple shrines where the spirits of nature and the dead were solicited by shamans. Third, around the fifth century, Imperial Household Shintoism *(Kōshitsu Shinto)*, in which rituals were performed by the emperor as shaman, emerged. Fourth, Primitive Shintoism and Shrine Shintoism absorbed Buddhism, Confucianism, the Way of Yin and Yang, and Taoism (which had previously been accepted from China) to bring forth two varieties: Doctrinal Shintoism *(Kyōka Shinto)*, professed by scholars and learned circles, and eclectic Folk Shintoism *(Minkan Shinto)*, which appealed to the common people. These are the premodern types of Shintoism.

In the early Meiji period (1876–1912), under the initiative of the central government, Shrine Shintoism was amalgamated with Imperial Household Shintoism to produce a powerful doctrine of State Shinto. After the 1868 overthrow of the Tokugawa regime, the group surrounding the Meiji Emperor perceived that to unify the country, then divided into some 270 fiefs, a strong ideology and national symbol were urgently needed. That was the genesis of State Shintoism, which is a modern specimen. The deepest division now lies between State Shintoism, on the one hand, and eclectic Folk Shintoism, on the other.

In 1868, in order to make the distinction between Shintoism and Buddhism clear, the government ordered Shinto shrines to be purged of Buddhist images and paraphernalia. This resulted in violence between the "destroy Buddha" Shintoist priests and the devout Buddhist believers. This anti-Buddhist policy deviated from the traditional Shintoist attitude toward religion, which was clearly tolerant and nonexclusive. The government finally ruled that State Shintoism was not a religion but was *above* and *beyond* all religions. This permitted the freedom of conscience later guaranteed in the Constitution of 1889. The ban on Christianity had been lifted in 1873, and the government took steps at the same time to put an end to the "destroy Buddha" campaign. This episode is very significant, for it reveals how strongly and deeply Buddhism took root among the Japanese people, being fused with Folk Shintoism, which was by nature eclectic.

Emperor worship is at the core of State Shintoist dogma,

explicitly expressed in the Imperial Rescript on Education issued in 1890 and taught to all youngsters through compulsory moral education at the primary-school level. It teaches that the emperor is divine because of his unbroken lineage from the sun goddess Amaterasu. It emphasizes that the emperor is the father and the empress is the mother of all Japanese, and that the imperial household is the main family from which all Japanese families have branched out. Thus, loyalty to the emperor is identified with filial piety to one's own parents. Loyalty to the emperor demands willingness to die for his sake should a national emergency arise.

Let me point out the distinctive features of Folk Shintoism in contrast to State Shintoism. First, Folk Shintoism is primarily nature worship, based on a belief in a symbiotic relationship between man and nature. This belief continues an animistic view that endows trees, animals, plants, mountains, water, fields, and stones with spirits similar to those of human beings. Second, Folk Shintoism worships the spirits of the dead; that is the basis for ancestor worship. The Japanese believe that the spirit of the deceased first goes to the hillside at the back of his or her house and that, as time passes, it gradually purifies itself until, thirty-three years after death, it becomes fused with the ancestral spirit of the family. They believe that communication between the living and the dead can be held at any time, not just on the special occasions of the two major festivals, Bon and New Year's. They believe that the unrealized aspirations of the dead should be carried out by succeeding generations so that unfinished tasks might be completed. This makes important the feelings and thoughts of a person's last moments, feelings and thoughts made known to the survivors so that the dying person's wishes may be fulfilled. In Buddhist teachings, on the other hand, the departed soul should leave this land of filth and enter the Pure Land, the quicker the better. Paradoxically, Buddhism, originally an anti-ancestor-worship religion, came to serve and reinforce Japanese ances-tor-worship. The Japanese attitude toward eclecticism is selective: they pick up foreign beliefs and then mold them to their own purposes.

In spite of the great effort on the part of the Meiji adminis-trators to inculcate the emperor ideology, there are some reasons to believe that the indoctrination was not as success-ful as it was supposed to be. Evidence that supports my contention is found in the messages of Japanese ex-officers and soldiers who were executed as war criminals by the International War Crimes Tribunal and other local trial courts outside Japan where most soldiers fought. Of the 1,068 who were executed or died in prison from 1946 to 1951, mostly class-B and class-C war criminals, 701 left letters, diaries, essays, or poems. Of these, *only forty-seven persons* openly avowed that they were dying for the sake of the Emperor. Among these forty-seven, some wrote that al-though they did not believe in dying for the Emperor they still should shout *banzai* for the Emperor at the moment of their death, lest their surviving families be shamed.

In this connection, it is apropos to say a few words about the Yasukuni Shrine, which literally means "the shrine to safeguard the state." Its forerunner was the Shōkon-sha, established in 1869 to enshrine the spirits of the dead soldiers of the Imperial army who fought against the supporters of the shogunate. In 1879 the name Shōkon-sha was changed to Yasukuni Shrine and was endowed with the status of a "government shrine." Since then, all the dead soldiers who fought in the Sino-Japanese War, the Russo-Japanese War, and the fifteen-year war from 1931 to 1945 have been en-shrined as the "guardian gods of the state." The whole pur-pose of the Yasukuni Shrine was the glorification of death on the battlefield for the sake of the emperor. However, very few messages of the ex-soldiers specifically referred to the Yasukuni Shrine as their souls' final destination. On the other hand, more than 180 expressed their belief that their spirits, after death, would return to watch over their ancestral land *(sokoku)* or their families or both. As for the place of the spirits' repose, the common reference was to "the top of the hill at the back of my house" rather than to the Yasukuni Shrine. Looking at these data it seems clear that the Folk Shintoist belief in ancestor worship far outweighs the State Shintoist precept of dying for the emperor.

Another interesting feature was that the men who expected that their spirits would return to their ancestral land or to their families also expected that their spirits would go either to the Christian heaven or to the Buddhist Pure Land or both. Such a fascinating mixture shows the tolerant religious attitude characteristic of eclectic Folk Shintoism.

After World War II the Emperor suddenly declared himself to be human, not divine. The Constitution of 1947 defined the Emperor as the "symbol of national unity" instead of the sovereign (as declared in the Constitution of 1889). The compulsory school courses in morality and ethics based on the Imperial Rescript on Education were abolished. Article 20 of the new postwar Constitution prohibits religious bodies from receiving any privileged position from the government. Accordingly, the Yasukuni Shrine was deprived of its previous status and became a private religious organization. Thus State Shintoism lost its key elements.

What about the youth born and educated after World War II? In a survey of 2,000 young people between the ages of eighteen and twenty-four from eleven countries including Japan, conducted by the prime minister's office, less than 20 percent of the Japanese responded "yes" to the question "Do you have a religion?" (Of those, 0.6 percent chose Catholicism, 1.1 percent Protestantism, 12.7 percent Buddhism, 0.9 percent Shintoism, and 4 percent other religions. This was in marked contrast to the replies given by American, British, West German, Swiss, Indian, Filipino, and Brazilian youth,

90 percent of whom gave a positive reply.) In a similar survey conducted in 1975, although the majority of the young people denied the "transcendental existence of God or Buddha," the majority also emphatically and positively responded to "respect for life," "respect for and fear of nature," "meaningfulness of prayer," and "ancestor worship."

Pulling these surveys together reveals two trends that are characteristic of today's Japanese youth: (1) they are not interested in institutionalized religions, but they are interested in religious attitudes and the content of religious beliefs; (2) they do not consider themselves Shintoists, but what they claim to believe is very close to the contents of Folk Shintoist beliefs, such as "ancestor worship" and "respect for and fear of nature." Folk Shintoist rites are prevalent in urban life. It is still customary for parents in cities as well as in towns and villages to bring a baby one hundred days after its birth to the *ujigami,* the native shrine, to ask the guardian deity for protection. When it is time for Japanese to marry, they have a wide variety of weddings to choose from: Shintoist, Christian, or no religious ceremony. Even though the bride and bridegroom may not be Christian, they can, if they prefer, have a wedding in a church. Christian weddings are quite popular among urban youth. However, for funerals, Buddhist priests are usually called in, perhaps because the surviving members of the family need to hear the Buddhist chanting to fully accept the death of the deceased.

It seems that complex factors, bearing not only on the national scene but also on international relations, will determine whether narrow-minded nationalism, fermented by State Shintoism, will be stirred up again, or whether the ecumenical attitude of mixing with other religions, international open-mindedness, and ecologically sound concepts of symbiosis between man and nature as embodied in Folk Shintoism will thrive.

4

The Japanese Economy in the World

Foreword

By now much has been said and written about Japan's stupendous economic performance and America's own lackluster showing over the past decade. Whatever one may say about the pros and cons of this issue, one thing is certain: in sheer volume there has never been an international trade the likes of that between the United States and Japan. In 1978 Japan's economy grew by 5.6 percent, as compared to 4 percent for the United States, 3.4 percent for Germany, 3.3 percent for France, and 3 percent for the United Kingdom. In terms of inflation, the consumer price index jumped 7.7 percent in the United States (low enough to be a pleasant memory in view of what has happened since then!) and only 5.5 percent in Japan. Japan's trade surplus with the United States was about $10.1 billion, and with the European community about $5 billion, although the monthly average surplus dropped to $600 million in 1979 from $1.4 billion in 1978. While 1980 hit all the industrialized nations hard, and while Japan's trade surplus has since turned into a deficit as consumer prices have begun to rise faster than in previous years, the newest statistics do not alter the general concern over the economic relationship of the United States with Japan. Prime Minister Ōhira pledged to open Japan's domestic market to foreign imports and to render the Japanese economy more hospitable to American firms. Other knowledgeable observers, like discussant Ezra Vogel and panelist Yotaro Kobayashi, have asserted that productivity in other countries could

be increased by learning from Japan and that American corporations should exert themselves more to break into the
Japanese domestic market.

There is still a school of thought which maintains that
serious weaknesses can be detected behind Japan's apparent
economic strength. Among such vulnerabilities discussant
Hugh Patrick included (1) Japan's vulnerability to military
attack, (2) its lack of raw materials, (3) its very trading structure, which makes it vulnerable to political pressure from
nations to whom it exports on a large scale, and (4) its paro-
chialism in an interdependent world. The Japanese see themselves as weak, as simply responding to world events, and
therefore they sometimes appear to other nations to be advo-
cates of a narrowly defined self-interest. But there are also
those who see too many parallels between American and
Japanese development to accept so pat an argument. Panelist
Kazuo Nukazawa, for one, emphasized that both economies
are becoming services-oriented at a comparable pace, with
very large proportions of employment and production being
diverted to the tertiary sector. In the long run, he felt, this
trend would make Japan less vulnerable. Mr. Nukazawa
added that Japan has on occasion changed economic policy
in response to foreign pressure. Patrick put it a bit more
forcefully when he pointed out that Japanese bureaucrats
have been effective in utilizing foreign pressures as a mechanism for resolving domestic political problems, making the
United States a scapegoat in that process. In all this, consumers are rarely mentioned. Both sides—the economic protec-
tionists and those demanding that Japan open its doors wider
—indulge in scapegoating. Japanese apologists in government and in the press argue that Japan is under pressure to
import more in order to satisfy American demands, without
mentioning the fact that such liberalized imports may also
benefit the average Japanese citizen and consumer. On the

other hand, Americans have a corresponding blind spot when it comes to their own corporations' lack of competitive spirit, and accuse Japan of exporting unemployment when the cause of the unemployment at home may in fact be more complex.

The term "Japan Inc." has come to be used as an epithet by foreign businessmen. Discussant Paul Finney noted that, while Japan Inc. exists, it simply means that Japanese corporations are a profit-making extension of Japan's society in general, implying that in Japan there is a smoother coordination between the two than in the United States. It seems that Japanese decision-makers should begin to take their citizens' welfare more seriously, and that American decision-makers must stop carping and start selling. There is a world of progress and prosperity to be gained from a healthy mix of cooperation and competition on both sides.

Japan and the United States: Economic Counterparts
EISUKE SAKAKIBARA

Past analyses of the Japanese economy, particularly in the United States, have tended to emphasize the uniqueness or the peculiarities of Japanese economy and society, and perhaps rightly so. One could look at the situation from that perspective, but I think that Japan is not an exotic and peculiar country in the Orient, but just another affluent industrialized country like the Western European countries and the United States. And if anything, Japan is very much like the United States.

Because of the emphasis on Japan's uniqueness, three major aspects of the total picture have been overlooked. First, Japan and the United States are probably the two industrialized countries with the most competitive markets in the world. In technical terms, Japan has a market structure that could be called oligopolistic. In oligopolistic competition, the cost of market entry is a bit high both for the domestic producers and for foreign producers, and this has become a recent source of trouble between Japan and the United States. But within this market structure there has been fierce and severe competition, and it is precisely because of this competition that Japan was able to achieve a very high rate of growth. There has been a widespread notion, particularly in the United States, that government controls and administered guidance are behind the Japanese economy's high rate of growth. That is a misconception. The ratio of government expenditure to GNP in 1975 was around 25.7 percent in Japan, as compared to 36 percent in the United States, 45.8 percent in the United Kingdom, and 45.7 percent in Germany. People have often claimed that the reason for the Japanese government's low ratio of expenditure to GNP is low defense spending, and it is true that Japanese defense expenditure is quite low, 0.9 percent of the GNP. But even when we take that defense expenditure into account, the picture is essentially the same. The ratio of defense expenditure to GNP in the United States is only 6 percent; if we add that percentage to the Japanese ratio of government expenditure to GNP, we still have around 30 percent—several percentage points less than for the United States and 15 percent less than for the European countries. In quantitative terms there is no question that Japan has maintained the least government spending of all the industrialized countries.

People might claim, however, that what they imply by "Japan Inc." is basically qualitative. They might point to government subsidies and the implicit guardian role of the government. But if one checks sector by sector, the areas where the government still has strong leverage are quite limited. One area is petroleum. The Ministry of International Trade and Industry (MITI) still has considerable influence on that industry, based on the 1962 Petroleum Industry Act. Another area is the public corporations, Nippon Telephone and Telegraph (NTT), Japan National Railways, and the Japan Monopoly Corporation (the tobacco industry). Other such sectors are banking, securities, and agriculture. But the ratio of Japan's controlled sectors to the entire economy is relatively low, and it is certainly lower than the ratio prevailing in Europe. I would like to emphasize that the motor manufacturing sector, which is a bastion of Japanese export, is highly competitive. Such competitiveness is exemplified by corporate rebellion in Japan; even in the 1950s and 1960s such rebellion existed. One notable example is Sumitomo in the late 1950s, which resisted MITI's administrative guidance. Another example is Sharp, the calculator producer that rebelled against MITI in the 1970s and whose products nevertheless now flood the market.

The second major aspect that has been overlooked is the fact that the United States and Japan are probably two of the most egalitarian and socially mobile countries in the industrialized world. Both enjoy a high quality of life and affluence. There have been some misconceptions about the quality of life in Japan; there have been some European stories about Japanese workaholics living in rabbit hutches, and it is true that housing is very tight in Tokyo. But these are problems typical of all large cities, and housing in New York is not that good either—nor is housing in Paris, where rent is exorbitant. In fact, as far as housing is concerned, Japan and the United States probably rank highest among the industrialized countries of the world. The ratio of home ownership to the total number of houses is about 65 percent in the United States, and around 60 percent in Japan, as compared to 50 percent in the United Kingdom and 35 percent in Germany. So despite exorbitant prices for land and housing, more than half of Japanese families do own their own homes.

The implication of this statistic is that the average Japanese worker earns a very good income. In 1979 Japanese workers earned, on the average, about $5.50 an hour, a wage generally comparable to an American worker's. In addition, Japanese enjoy large fringe benefits, such as the retirement lump sum which, for a typical university graduate who has served a company for thirty-five years, would amount to about $70,000. Ordinary workers in large corporations usually enjoy a subsidy for housing that probably averages $50,000 per person. As for medical care, there are various ways to measure its efficiency. The average stay of a hospital patient is as long as thirty-five days in Japan, as compared to eight days in the United States. This seems to show an abundance of hospital space and medical care and a lower cost for hospital administration in Japan. Another area of social welfare is pensions, and Japan presently pays some of the highest pensions in the world. The ordinary pension is around $500 a month per couple, roughly equivalent to the amounts paid in the Scandinavian countries and Germany.

The third neglected aspect of Japan's economy is the diffuseness of the nation's decision-making mechanism. It has mistakenly been thought, both in Japan and abroad, that the country's economic decisions are made in a highly centralized fashion. In fact, however, Japan is a kind of federation of various organizations, each vying with the others for autonomy. Those with some experience negotiating with the Japanese government have noticed that each ministry's desire for autonomy is so strong that interministerial feuds often interfere with administrative efficiency. The same type of inter-organizational struggle exists between the private sector and the public sector; under the superficial guise of compliance, private companies struggle for autonomy from the government.

In sum, (1) Japan and the United States are characterized by highly competitive markets that are unique among the industrialized countries of the world; (2) Japan and the United States both have very high social mobility and a basically egalitarian social structure, whereas European countries are characterized by the remnants of a highly stratified class society; and (3) the Japanese decision-making mechanism is characterized by diffuseness. In each of these three areas there are problems for both countries. As far as competitive markets are concerned, the proliferation of government intervention in the name of environmental and consumer protection could threaten the effective working of the market mechanism. And the tax system and social welfare system have reached a stage where both countries are experiencing some glut and people are beginning to question the basic justice and fairness of the present arrangements. Still another problem is the lack of leadership. The United States and Japan seem to have much in common, both positive and negative, and both could benefit from increasing interdependence, so long as they do not forget that they share common objectives and interests in the maintenance of a dynamic and competitive market.

The Business Environment in Japan Today
YOTARO KOBAYASHI

Japanese businessmen are seeing important changes taking place today, particularly in contrast to the environment that existed in the 1960s and early 1970s. Yet much remains to be done about United States–Japan trade frictions.

Recently I had a visit from the head of a multinational company which is based on the West Coast and has been growing at a rate of 50 to 70 percent a year in a computer-oriented peripheral field. This particular company now enjoys something like 60 to 70 percent of the market in its field. Its president had been in Japan discussing some business with his licensee there, Matsushita Electric Company. Although he was very proud of his own company's high productivity, visiting Matsushita factories completely changed his mind. He told me that Matsushita is at least four times more productive than his company. Similarly, about a year ago a friend of mine in the textile industry in Japan told me that he had been invited to Korea to give technical advice on new textile equipment that a Korean company had installed. To his surprise the equipment was too modern for him to give advice about; he had never seen such equipment. Korea was way ahead in investment for modern manufacturing technologies in this area.

These examples deal with the issue of productivity. As far as Japan is concerned, important changes are now taking place in business. When Japanese firms were enjoying rapid growth in the 1960s, the base for such growth was provided by an ample, high-quality, well-educated labor force. Japan had an automatic supply of young labor that would supply creativity and imagination at relatively low cost. But this is no longer the case. We are actually seeing a fundamental change in the structure of the labor population. Japan is becoming an aging country at a speed much faster than the United States, Germany, or France. One important factor in this process is the decrease in sources of labor from junior and senior high schools, in part the result of more people from those younger sectors continuing on to higher education. Slower economic growth in recent years has also slowed the rate of new hiring, cutting down on certain job opportunities and therefore inducing students to stay in school a little longer. The average life expectancy of both males and females has also been increasing dramatically, so that many companies are now extending the compulsory retirement age (which used to be 55) to 57, 60, or 65, which is quite natural when life expectancy is over 70.

What kinds of things are Japanese businesses doing to maintain productivity? For one thing, they are changing the wage system, which used to be a straightforward seniority wage system that paid higher wages according to age and length of employment. A structured labor force the average age of which increases automatically every year will ultimately kill a company because of the constantly rising overhead cost. Significant changes are beginning to be made in this area. For example, many companies are introducing a first cutoff point at about age thirty-five, beyond which the seniority system will not apply. Some of the companies are introducing a system whereby people at or over the age of forty have to go through a stage of reeducation and retesting. They are taken out of their jobs for six months or a year to be reeducated and retrained for new jobs and new challenges; of course, not all will make the grade. These are some of the changes being made by Japanese business to maintain productivity, an absolute necessity because of the dependence on imported raw materials, particularly in the energy field. Unfortunately, there is little likelihood that this dependence will change in the future.

Productivity is an important issue to American industry as well. As *Fortune* magazine clearly indicated some time ago, there have been considerable differences in productivity between the United States and Japan since about 1960 in major segments of the economy. Unless something can be done to rectify this problem, the trade imbalance between the two countries will be chronic. There can be short-term remedies, political or otherwise, but as long as this productivity gap remains, the trade imbalance will not disappear. There is a limit to how much more Japan can open its domestic market, because there are already few barriers to speak of. American business should aggressively explore marketing opportunities in Japan. Fuji Xerox, Japan IBM, and Coca-Cola demonstrate that there are many successes in Japan, and they have been around for some time. They came in at a time when regulations were tighter, when people knew less, relatively speaking, about the rest of the world, and they have earned their positions by imagination, creativity, and hard work. I think these cases are, and should be, encouraging signs for American business, indicating that such things can still be achieved in Japan. Too much is made of the mythical Japanese market, the notion that Japanese consumers are different and prefer Japanese goods to those of foreign make. They are there to be persuaded, but American businessmen have not made enough of an effort. I return to the example of my American friend who marveled at Matsushita's high productivity. He went on to say that he felt there was a great deal to be learned from Matsushita, and I am confident that others can do something similar to what Matsushita is doing. This is the kind of positive attitude that is necessary and that characterized American business some years back. The fact that the Japanese do not see this often enough anymore is very unfortunate.

One might well ask what have been the key factors in Japanese business to cause such high productivity. I would simply mention two things. First, for a long time the Japanese did as the Korean textile company mentioned above did: invested aggressively in modern manufacturing technology. In the case of Matsushita, it even has a special division employing a few hundred people who specialize exclusively in studying and introducing modern manufacturing technologies. They provide service to the other divisions of the whole group. The second factor is probably more important. This is a question of people. In Japan employment system practices have been different from those in the United States. There is much less turnover; people stay with one employer for a longer period of time. In addition, a number of leading Japanese companies, including Toyota, Matsushita, Bridgestone, and Hitachi, have been employing certain management techniques designed to make the whole body of workers a cohesive group that will work toward a common goal, from the president down to the workers on the floor and the salesmen on the street. This is probably "Japan Inc." in its purest form.

It is this system that Korea is trying to introduce on a national basis. Over the last five or six years the Korean government has hired a group of professors from Japan (who have been very successful in helping a number of Japanese companies to reach their present levels of productivity) to apply the same mechanism and methods on a national scale. When we discussed this with our American friends some time ago, even the friends at Xerox felt that this approach would not work in the United States, that people are different here. They would not work hand in hand with people in other jobs. I cannot believe Americans are that different. There can be much improvement in this approach, not only in pure quantitative productivity but also in a greater degree of job satisfaction on the part of the workers. It is absolutely necessary for Japan and the United States to maintain a healthy trade relationship. Otherwise they will both be on the same side of the fence trying to fight against a common adversary at the same time that they are obstructing each other's progress.

5

Politics in Japan

Foreword

It has been said many times that Japan's stable democratic order is an extraordinary accomplishment. In some respects Japan's democratic institutions resemble those in continental European systems, but the American Occupation and its aftermath have complicated the issue by transforming Japan's democracy into a hybrid of European and American models. In addition, the Japanese political system has some unique features, such as the multimember districts with single-vote elections, or the division (noted by panelist Tasuku Asano in this part) between the ruling Liberal Democratic Party's performance of an effectiveness function and the opposition parties' fulfillment of the legitimacy function of government. This clear-cut division of labor has begun to disintegrate, and there are growing signs of strain within the Japanese body politic. The Japanese have never warmed to the idea of winner take all, and as long as the opposition parties at least have a chance to be heard, stability can probably be maintained.

But some of the strains now being experienced by Japan's political system are similar to those occurring in democratic systems everywhere. One such international phenomenon is the growth of that group of citizens who classify themselves as independents, as nonsupporters of any particular political party. A 1976 survey of Tokyo voters recorded that 40 percent of those in their early twenties called themselves independents, and they constituted the largest single bloc of those voting. This is certainly comparable to the trend toward independent voting in the United States.

Another similarity between Japan and the West was pointed out by discussant Herbert Passin: not only the Liberal Democratic Party (LDP), but virtually every ruling party in every parliamentary system of the advanced industrial nations has suffered a similar decline of popular support. However, another discussant, George Packard, took issue with Asano and others who predict an early death for the LDP, and cited as contrary evidence the recent conservative victories in the gubernatorial elections in Tokyo and Osaka, two cities that have for many years been safe wins for the opposition progressives.

There are other political tensions within Japan today that are not unique to that country. Discussant Bernard Silberman specified two: the tension between the local governments and Tokyo, and the tension between interests treated as legitimate and those given short shrift. In the former case, Japanese local government remains suspicious of a central bureaucracy whose long-range plans often seem to result in the sacrifice of local interests for the sake of some national goal. In the latter case, labor is not represented in Japan at the central government level. Moreover, the enterprise unions that embrace the majority of workers represent permanent labor and therefore tend not to represent the interests of the large cohort of Japanese laborers who are employed as temporary workers in large-scale enterprises.

Although it may be argued that affluence is a necessary prerequisite for a healthy democratic system, that affluence or its consequences also engender stresses which inhibit the smooth performance of that system. Money has indeed been blamed for much of what is wrong with Japan's democracy, so much so that Yoshio Murakami, one of the panelists, coined the word "moneycracy" to describe a political arena in which the main event is the exchange of huge sums of untraceable cash. The unlimited flow of that cash to the LDP has been somewhat slowed by the revision of the campaign financing law under Prime Minister Miki, which significantly limited the ability of industrial organizations and corporations to make political contributions. There are differences from the United States not only in the collection of political funds but in the uses of such funds. The strict election campaign laws prohibit politicians from buying time on commercial television for political advertising. What limited media exposure is permitted is provided free to all candidates. The same laws also prohibit campaigning earlier than thirty days before an election, but in fact politicians evade this restriction and campaign for as much as a year before the actual election takes place. This, of course, means that all politicians are knowingly breaking the law, which does not enhance their image in the eyes of the Japanese public, who are well known for their jaundiced view of politicians in general. Such laws also present a potential danger in the opportunity they offer to police and government officials to harass individual politicians for infractions of rules that everyone acknowledges are unrealistic and are bound to encourage noncompliance in the first place. This also contributes to the Japanese public's discomfort with democratic elections and electioneering.

Japan is at present experiencing a heavy dose of the same alienating and disorienting tendencies that all Western democracies are now undergoing, and it may well be that Japan's greatest asset in trying to deal with these problems will be traditional values—not of obedience, endurance, and authoritarianism but of compromise, consensus, and acceptance of the fact that people cannot always have everything in life they want. One of Japan's major frustrations has arisen because the Japanese have tried to overcome such a traditional attitude and the limitations it inevitably dictates. The underlying theme in Japanese political behavior on the world scene has been the desire for self-sufficiency, and the very impossibility of that goal has in no small way contributed to the present government's dilemma.

Postwar Japanese Politics
KAN ORI

Japan has a parliamentary system somewhat like that of the United Kingdom but with some American features as well, such as an independent Supreme Court with the right of judicial review and the functionally specific standing committees in the Diet. These are, of course, the American Occupation influences. American political scientist E. E. Schattschneider once described the American party system as a truncated pyramid. He argued that in the United States there are state and local parties which are real parties but that there is no national party, which he called a ghost party. The Japanese political party organizations are somewhat similar in that they are to some extent ghost parties. This ghost has no legs or feet: Japan's parties have national organizations but lack a grass-roots base. That lack of grass-roots involvement is one of the chief characteristics of the Japanese political party system, and therefore party identification tends to be weak. Neither is there party-ticket voting like that in the United States. What kind of organizations substitute for grass-roots support? One is the *kōenkai*—a personal support organization—and the other is the intraparty faction. The *kōenkai* is very much like the home office of an American congressman but with the distinct difference that the constituents are encouraged to channel their demands indirectly through the local *kōenkai* rather than contacting the Diet member directly. Every Liberal Democratic Party member in the Diet, according to political scientist Masao Soma and others, has his own individual *kōenkai.* In the case of the Socialists, the unions serve such a function, except for those Socialists who come from a Japan Farmers' Union background, who have their own *kōenkai.* In a nutshell, the *kōenkai* is a mass-based individual electoral support mechanism.

Another element is the factions, which function like major political party organizations elsewhere and are characteristic of all Japanese political parties except the Kōmeitō. The Liberal Democratic Party (LDP) has had eight to thirteen factions (five major ones currently), and the Japan Socialist Party also has several factions of varied shades of Socialist orientation. In 1960 it was from the Japan Socialist Party that the right-wing Nishio faction splintered off to form the present Democratic Socialist Party. Scholars have discussed various causes of factionalism in Japanese politics. Important among them are historical tradition, electoral arrangements (three- to five-men districts for the House of Representatives), and election of the party head, particularly that of the LDP president. Regardless of causes, two points are salient. First, although Socialist party factionalism has ideological overtones, the factional relationship in Japan is primarily personal and direct, based upon personal allegiance owed to an individual leader, not to the faction as such or to the party as a whole. The second point to be noted is that the intraparty faction in Japan functions very much like an independent party elsewhere. For example, Liberal Democratic Party candidates are recruited through intraparty factions, and usually no faction puts up more than one candidate per district. Thus, several LDP (conservative) candidates who represent the different factions may be running for election in the same district. Japan has a three- to five-man district arrangement, with one exception (Amami, which is a single-member district), and has plurality election but a single-vote ballot. Under these circumstances it is natural that election campaigns are conducted along factional lines, particularly in predominantly conservative districts. Meanwhile, factional leaders are not only instrumental in recruiting candidates for party nomination but also responsible for providing campaign funds as well as organizational aid. Furthermore, it is factional affiliation that determines advancement both in appointive government posts and in the party hierarchy, for it is believed that a judicious balance of factions must be maintained among all Cabinet posts, political vice-ministerships, committee chairmen in the Diet, and all party offices. Even in the Japan Socialist Party, factional alignment is quite important in the selection of party officials. Finally, it is factional coalitions of the Liberal Democratic Party that in essence determine who becomes the prime minister of Japan, because as the president of the ruling majority party in the Diet—at least for the time being—he is usually elected automatically as the premier.

Not only are there *kōenkai* and factions, but there is also the relationship between the public bureaucracy and the Liberal Democratic Party to consider. Though its major support is in rural areas, the Liberal Democratic Party primarily represents the interests of Japanese business, particularly big business. It is well known that the big-business community provides the LDP with a great deal of, if not almost all, its political funds. A considerable portion of that is given through the People's Political Association (Kokumin Seiji Kyōkai) to the party headquarters, but the rest is channeled directly to various faction leaders or to individual Diet members. While each faction has its own sponsors, the Japanese business community seems to have favored what are known as bureaucratic factions, those factions led by former higher civil servants. One should note that for some time retiring members of the Japanese higher bureaucracy have been the major source of supply for LDP membership in the Diet. This pattern started in 1953 and continues to this day (two other areas, the public corporation and the business world, are also popular post-retirement careers for the higher bureaucracy). Accordingly, one out of every four Liberal Democrats in the House of Representatives and more than one out of every three newly elected in the House of Councillors have been former higher civil servants. Not only do these ex-bureaucrats-turned-politicians comprise a large segment of LDP membership in the Diet but also they are important leaders of the government and the party. Their close contacts with incumbent bureaucrats, their expertise in public policy, and their first-rate financial connections, which are indispensable for the faction leaders, enable them to rise rapidly in the hierarchy. Significantly, for only a very few of the thirty-odd years of postwar Cabinet history have Cabinets been headed by prime ministers who did not have bureaucratic backgrounds. For example, from 1955 to 1979, over 40 percent of Japanese Cabinet ministers have been former higher civil servants. Other sources of recruitment for the Liberal Democratic Party are assistants to Diet members, and what are called *bankisha* (reporters who are assigned to cover specific political figures), as well as politicians who climb up from local assemblies or prefectural assemblies. But I would emphasize the predominance of ex-bureaucrats in the LDP leadership positions. Their numbers are overwhelming—as much as lawyers in American politics are.

The bureaucracy, of course, has close connections with business as well, and people talk about this conservative triple alliance among the LDP, big business, and the higher bureaucracy. In contrast, the Japan Socialist Party speaks for labor, particularly organized labor. In fact, it primarily represents the interests of a single-interest group called the General Council of Trade Unions of Japan, known in Japanese as Sōhyō. Although there are other union federations, Sōhyō is by far the largest federation of labor, with 4.5 million members, and most of the unions come from the public sector. Accordingly, more than one-half of the Socialist members of the House of Representatives in recent years have been labor officials. A similar trend can be detected in the House of Councillors. Even if they are not Sōhyō-related, many members of the Japan Socialist Party owe a great deal to the Sōhyō unions, in that Sōhyō members constitute about 70 percent of the Socialist Party membership—enough to control conventions—and Sōhyō raises almost all the party's campaign funds. The Democratic Socialist Party is in a similar situation, although it does not represent a single interest per se but essentially represents the interests of Dōmei (the Japanese Confederation of Labor), which has over 2 million members. Similarly, Kōmeitō is the political arm of the religious organization called Sōkagakkai, which has claimed a family membership of about 8 million in recent years. Although Sōkagakkai and Kōmeitō are ostensibly separate— and in fact officially severed relations in 1970 after the freedom-of-the-press controversy—almost all the workers, leaders, and candidates of Kōmeitō are members of Sōkagakkai. It is difficult to distinguish members of Sōkagakkai from members of Kōmeitō because identical persons play dual roles in both organizations, and the two organizations and their leadership are closely interlocked.

The public bureaucracy has essentially three major characteristics. The first is the elitist nature of the higher civil service in Japan, which is quite different from that of the American civil service. It is perhaps somewhat similar to the British senior administrative class. The members of the public bureaucracy are well educated and very capable people, with more than 80 percent of the first- and second-grade officers in the public service in the postwar era coming from Tokyo University. They also pass stiff higher civil service examinations. The second major characteristic is the political nature of the Japanese bureaucracy. In addition to the afore-mentioned tendency of ex-bureaucrats to migrate into poli-tics upon retirement, there exists a legacy of political involvement by the higher civil service in Japan. In fact, they have been the movers of modern Japan. Whereas in the United States the merit system was developed to counter the political spoils system, in Japan political involvement with the bureaucracy was there from the beginning. The third, and perhaps the most important, characteristic is that the members of the Japanese bureaucracy are policy specialists. They make policy rather than deal with the details of ad-ministration. It is important to note the lack of political con-trol by political appointees over the higher bureaucracy. The reason for this is that the Japanese Cabinet is formulated on the basis of factional considerations, as already mentioned, so that the average tenure of ministers is about eight to nine months, and one can hardly gain control of the bureaucracy in such a short period of time.

The accompanying table shows three major features of mass political participation and patterns of party support from 1947 to 1979: (1) The continued dominance of the conservatives, the LDP, from 1955 on. They won about 60 percent of the popular vote and seats. (2) During the same period the combined Socialist forces did not get more than 36 percent of the vote in elections for the House of Repre-sentatives. The Japan Socialist Party itself was no more than a third party. (3) If the election of 1949 is excluded, the impact of parties other than the major ones has been insig-nificant for these years, especially since the conservative party merger in 1955. The 1967 general election for the House of Representatives is significant because it marks the beginning of a new trend toward a multiparty pattern called *tatōka* in Japan, at least in the opposition camp. In that elec-

RESULTS OF POSTWAR GENERAL ELECTIONS FOR THE HOUSE
OF REPRESENTATIVES, JAPAN, 1947–76

Election	LDP[a]	JSP[b]	DSP[c]	JCP[d]	Kōmeitō[e]	New Liberal Club	Minor Parties	Independent
			Percentage of House Seats					
1947	60.3	30.7	—	0.8	—	—	5.4	2.8
1949	74.5	10.3	—	7.5	—	—	5.1	2.6
1952	69.6	23.8	—	—	—	—	2.4	4.1
1953	66.5	29.6	—	0.2	—	—	1.3	2.4
1955	63.6	33.4	—	0.4	—	—	1.3	1.3
1958	61.5	35.5	—	0.2	—	—	0.2	2.6
1960	63.3	31.0	3.6	0.6	—	—	0.2	1.0
1963	60.6	30.8	4.9	1.0	—	—	—	2.7
1967	57.0	28.8	6.2	1.0	5.1	—	—	1.9
1969	59.3	18.5	6.4	2.9	9.7	—	—	3.2
1972	57.8	24.0	4.0	7.9	5.9	—	—	0.2
1976	48.7	24.0	6.0	3.6	11.0	3.6	0.0	4.1
1979	48.5	20.9	6.9	7.6	11.1	0.8	0.4	3.7
			Percentage of Popular Votes					
1947	58.9	26.2	—	3.7	—	—	5.4	5.8
1949	63.0	13.5	—	9.7	—	—	7.2	6.6
1952	66.1	21.2	—	2.6	—	—	3.4	6.7
1953	65.7	26.6	—	1.9	—	—	1.4	4.4
1955	63.2	29.2	—	2.0	—	—	2.3	3.3
1958	57.8	32.9	—	2.6	—	—	0.7	6.0
1960	57.5	27.5	8.7	2.9	—	—	0.3	2.8
1963	54.7	29.0	7.3	4.0	—	—	0.1	4.8
1967	48.8	27.9	7.4	4.8	5.4	—	0.4	5.4
1969	47.6	21.5	7.7	6.8	10.9	—	0.2	5.3
1972	46.8	21.9	7.0	10.5	8.5	—	0.3	5.0
1976	41.8	20.7	6.3	10.4	10.9	4.1	0.1	5.7
1979	44.6	19.7	6.8	10.4	9.8	3.0	0.8	4.9

[a]From 1947 to 1955 inclusive, LDP stands for all the major conservative parties; since the 1958 election, it means the Liberal Democratic Party.
[b]From 1947 to 1955 inclusive, JSP stands for all the Socialist parties; since the 1958 election, it means the Japan Socialist Party.
[c]Democratic Socialist Party.
[d]Japan Communist Party.
[e]Clean Government Party.

tion, the Liberal Democratic Party fell below its consistent majority in popular support for the first time since its establishment in 1955, even though it still held 57 percent of the House seats. The Japan Socialist Party did not, however, gain proportionately to the loss of the LDP. Instead, its percentage of House seats declined from that of the previous election, marking the nadir in its popularity since its consolidation in 1955. Furthermore, while the Liberal Democratic Party and the Japan Socialist Party were thus losing, the Democratic Socialist Party, the Kōmeitō, and the Communist Party all increased their strength in the 1967 elections for the House of Representatives. This basic trend continues.

In conclusion, I would like to mention the citizens' movement in Japan, which I consider to be a syndrome of post-industrial societies like the United States and, to some degree, Japan, in which questions about the quality of life are raised. Like their American counterparts, the Japanese are finding existing political institutions inadequate, and this movement may be another avenue for their political expression. The citizens' movement finds outlets in various neighborhood associations, women's groups, and consumer groups. On the whole, I am optimistic about the future of Japanese politics. It has worked pretty well for thirty-odd years. One problem is the credibility of government leaders —scandal, to be more precise, which is quite isomorphic to that of the Watergate incident. But I trust that the Japanese people's support for the political party system will be sustained, even though individual political leaders—such as former Prime Minister Tanaka—may be disgraced.

The End of Stability?
TASUKU ASANO

I am not as sanguine as Professor Ori about the current political situation in Japan. Certain aspects of Japanese politics are undergoing a very important transition, which may have far-reaching effects on Japanese democracy in the years to come.

Postwar Japan has been known for its remarkable stability and almost miraculous economic performance, but some or all of the factors that contributed to such stability now seem to be gone, or at least fading from prominence. If postwar Japan's stability is explainable by such characteristics inherent in Japanese society as vertical social structure or consensual orientation, then there is little cause for concern, because those characteristics do not readily change. But the political manifestations of those characteristics can and will change. After all, Japanese were just as group-oriented in the militarist 1930s as they are today, and yet the politics of the country is quite different now from what it was then. Political sociologist Seymour Martin Lipset states that a political system is stable when it is effective and legitimate. Effectiveness means actual performance, to the extent that essential government functions are being satisfied in a political system, such as providing for economic security or economic welfare, for personal or national security. Effectiveness is essentially a bread-and-butter question. Legitimacy, on the other hand, involves the system's capacity to create and maintain a belief among the people that existing political institutions are the most appropriate ones for that society, and as such effectiveness and legitimacy are obviously inter-related. In some political systems effectiveness and legitimacy go together, but in democratic governments there are cases where these two requirements of political stability work at cross-purposes. In order to be effective, political power tends to be concentrated in certain segments of the governmental structure, particularly in the national execu-tive. This concentration of power may incite some to agitate for greater popular control or popular participation in the policymaking process, and if these demands are not re-strained the process itself can be paralyzed.

The year 1955 was a watershed in Japanese politics, for in that year the conservative forces merged into the Liberal Democratic Party (LDP), and the divided Socialist parties reunited into the Japan Socialist Party; other parties were insignificant. Some anticipated that this was the harbinger of a two-party system, in which responsible parties would al-ternate in the position of power, but that did not happen. What developed instead was a single-party government in a democratic institution where the opposition parties never had any share in national government. However, that did not necessarily make those opposition parties politically irrele-vant. What developed was a unique division of labor be-tween the political parties, in which the Liberal Democratic Party—the conservative party—specialized more or less in effectiveness whereas the opposition parties specialized in legitimacy.

What are the issues surrounding this division of labor? Until recently, Japanese politics involved five major issues, five deeply felt concerns of the Japanese people. First, very obviously, was the question of economic rehabilitation, and later on the question of economic growth. There was practi-cally a consensus in Japan on the need to go ahead with economic growth. Second was the question of alliance with the United States for the security of Japan. Most Japanese were aware of the need for American protection. The third issue involved the sense of national independence. More precisely, it involved the question of how dependent Japan should be on the United States. While feeling it necessary to ally with the United States for Japanese security, some Japanese were uncomfortable with the kind of dependence that this relationship represented. Fourth, there was the question of institutionalizing democracy in Japan. Many people were aware of the immaturity of those democratic institutions that had been introduced into Japan after World War II, and many felt that there was a need to further consolidate them. Finally, the fifth concern of the Japanese people was pacifism, a desire to rebuild the country essentially as a non-military power. The last three issues—independence, democratic consolidation, and pacifism—primarily involved the sense of legitimacy. These were some of the democratic and pacifist assumptions explicit in Japan's new postwar Constitution, and belief in the Constitution is the very source of the system's legitimacy.

In this set of issues, the first two—economic growth and national security—were effectiveness-related, and the LDP as the party in power was entrusted with implementing them. That was only natural. Less natural was the extent to which the opposition did not also address themselves to these effectiveness issues. Of course the Japan Socialist Party and other opposition parties were very critical of the U.S.-Japan Security Treaty, but they were less outspoken about the security treaty as such than about the question of Japan's dependent relationship with the United States. It was in the area of legitimacy issues that the opposition parties were most articulate. The LDP in this kind of setting almost disarmed itself ideologically and reduced politics to economics.

There were elements in the LDP who chose to take issue with some of these legitimacy-related issues by arguing for a military buildup, for the revision of the Constitution, and for some kind of modification of the imperial institution. Those right-wing elements in the LDP were silenced during this period, because if the party stressed these questions too much it was sure to lose an election. Although the LDP party platform calls for a revision of the Constitution, that has been pretty much a dead issue up to now.

The arrangement was as convenient as it was unique. Most of the Japanese who had these five concerns in their minds could see some of them responded to by the LDP, and the rest adopted by opposition parties. For example, it may not be so unusual that in Japan a voter might vote for the Japan Socialist Party because he knows that it will never be in a position of power. The very confidence that his support will not put the Japan Socialist Party in power encourages him to vote for it, because he is expecting that party to be articulate on some of those questions and to check the LDP from railroading bills through the Diet. Therefore the opposition's reason for being is not to offer itself as a realistic alternative to the LDP to head the government, but to articulate its positions on these legitimacy issues. In this unique division of labor the Japanese political system as a whole provided for both effectiveness and legitimacy.

This kind of arrangement is now gone, as is the stability it had ensured. For one thing, the LDP is no longer predominant. It may continue to be in a position of power for some time to come, if less firmly, but the trend is in the direction of a new plural system without a dominant political party, and that will be a new experience for Japanese democracy in the postwar era. In this new situation the rules of the game will be very different, but there are no established or agreed-upon rules to follow as yet. There is now a peculiar sense of having lost all landmarks and being confronted with an entirely new and unfamiliar landscape. The fact that the 1955 arrangement is gone is reflected in the increasing number of voters who say they do not support any party or who classify themselves as independents. Opinion polls now show one in three adults as being independent. This large cohort feels that the LDP does not provide effectiveness and that the opposition parties do not perform the legitimizing function. This is going to undermine seriously Japan's future political process.

Ironically, many of the causes of the disintegration of the 1955 arrangement arose from the very success of the LDP government or the success of the system itself—in other words, the culprit is none other than economic growth. In 1955 more than 40 percent of the working population were engaged in primary industry, whereas in 1977 the rate was 11.5 percent. In little more than twenty years a huge number of people from rural areas rushed into the cities, and the LDP —depending for its political support upon the rural areas— allowed many of its supporters to sneak by. The fact that these people came to live in cities, and also in a kind of postindustrialized social setup, makes their political profile somewhat different from what it used to be. Economic roles also gave rise to a new set of issues, such as pollution, urban overcrowding, industrial readjustment, and so on, and whereas the LDP was very effective in governing because it could address the grievances by expanding the pie, the sense of vulnerability has increased—oil shocks, trade frictions, occasional suspicion and hatred directed at Japan where the Japanese economy is said to be overconspicuous.

Economic growth has made Japan more independent in its relationship with the United States, but the U.S.–Japan alliance is only a part of the diplomatic constellation, and the Japanese government now says that it is pursuing an omnidirectional foreign policy. That is easier said than done. In this kind of situation the LDP, which used to reduce politics to economics, is now beginning to address itself also to legitimacy-related issues in a manner quite atypical. Many of the previous political taboos, such as outspoken advocacy of a greater military buildup and the question of the imperial institution, have been lifted. The severe international environment might drive Japan to adopt a more nationalistic attitude. Of course, however nationalistic Japan might become, it is impossible for it to be completely shut out of the international community because of economic interdependence. The question remains whether, in coming to terms with the rest of the world, Japan will do so with prudence or in bad temper, with tolerance or in a spirit of habitual assertion. Opposition parties are just as confused. Postwar democracy in Japan proved to be a successful experiment largely because until recently it did not face the dilemma between legitimacy and effectiveness inherent in democracy. Churchill once said, "Democracy is the worst form of government except all others," and now the Japanese are beginning to experience some of its worst aspects.

Appendix: Short Biographies of the Participants in "Japan Today"

PANEL 1
The Japanese Today: Changing Life-Patterns

*SUMIKO FURUYA IWAO, b. 1935
Professor of Social Psychology, Keio University, and Lecturer, University of Tokyo
Professor Iwao received her M.A. and Ph.D. degrees in psychology from Yale University after completing her B.A. at Keio University. She teaches at Keio but spent summer 1972 as visiting lecturer at the East-West Center in Honolulu. The author of numerous articles in English and Japanese on communications, social psychology, and aesthetics and personality, Professor Iwao has also translated into Japanese such important works as Kenneth Langston's *Political Socialization.*

*KAORU KOBAYASHI, b. 1931
Professor of International Management, Institute of Business Administration and Management
In addition to teaching, Professor Kobayashi has participated in a number of Japanese government missions to the United Kingdom and ASEAN countries, as well as consulting with the Japan Overseas Enterprise Association, Chase Manhattan Bank, Japan Air Lines, and other firms. His articles on international business and labor have appeared in *Fortune, Columbia Journal of World Business,* and other publications.

MASAO KUNIHIRO, b. 1930
Lecturer, College of Commerce and Industry, Sophia University, and newscaster, Nihon Television (NTV)

Note: The names of panelists whose presentations are included in this volume are marked by asterisks. Only those discussants mentioned in the text are listed here.

113

A pioneer in simultaneous interpreting in English and Japanese, Professor Kunihiro was a founder of Simul Press and a director of the Simul International Corporation. He has also been a special assistant to Takeo Miki, first as a legislative aide when Miki was foreign minister and later as private political adviser on foreign affairs when he became prime minister.

Discussants: Solomon Levine, Professor of Labor Relations, University of Wisconsin; Ezra Vogel, Professor of Sociology, Harvard University.

PANEL 2
Japan: The Search for Identity

NAGAYO HOMMA, b. 1929
Professor of American History and Dean of the Graduate School of Sociology, University of Tokyo
An author of articles in both Japanese and English, Professor Homma has published (in Japanese) *Main Currents of Postwar American Politics* and edited a volume entitled *Lifestyles and Values.* After receiving his B.A. from the University of Tokyo, he did graduate work on American civilization and history at Amherst College and Columbia University before returning to the University of Tokyo, where he has taught ever since.

*AKIRA IRIYE, b. 1934
Professor of History and Chairman of the Department of Far Eastern Languages and Literature, University of Chicago
Professor Iriye was educated in the United States. He majored in English History at Haverford College, where he was a member of Phi Beta Kappa, and received his Ph.D. from Harvard University in American and Far Eastern History. After teaching at Harvard, the University of California at Santa Cruz, and the University of Rochester, he joined the faculty at the University of Chicago in 1969. He was also recipient of Woodrow Wilson and Guggenheim fellowships. Professor Iriye is the author and editor of numerous books on American and Far Eastern diplomatic history. His most recent publication is *U.S.–Asian Relations during the 1940s.*

*YOSHIKAZU SAKAMOTO, b. 1927
Professor of International Politics, University of Tokyo
A specialist in international politics, Professor Sakamoto has written several books in Japanese, including *Peace—Its Realities and Re-*

search, as well as numerous articles on foreign policy, ideology, and political forecasting. He has been a Rockefeller Fellow at Princeton University, an Eisenhower Fellow, and a Special Fellow at UNITAR. Professor Sakamoto was educated at the University of Tokyo.

Discussants: John Campbell, Professor of Political Science, University of Michigan; Richard Halloran, Washington bureau and former Tokyo correspondent, *New York Times.*

PANEL 3
Japanese Culture: Continuity and Change

SHUJI TAKASHINA, b. 1932
Associate Professor of Art History, University of Tokyo
An art historian and critic, Professor Takashina began his career as curator at the National Museum of Western Art in Tokyo, following study at the University of Paris and the Louvre. He has lectured and done research in the United States as a JDR 3rd Fund Fellow, in England as a guest of the British Academy, and in Paris at the Pompidou Center. His publications include *Art in Japan Today* (in English) and *History of Modern Painting* (in Japanese).

*KAZUKO TSURUMI, b. 1918
Professor of Sociology, Sophia University
Professor Tsurumi has taught at Stanford University, the University of British Columbia, the University of Toronto, and Princeton University. She has received many fellowships and grants to support her research and publications on values, modernization, and social change. Professor Tsurumi is the author of *Social Change and the Individual: Japan Before and After Defeat in World War II.* A graduate of Tsuda College, she did her graduate work at Vassar College and Princeton University, where she received her Ph.D. in Sociology in 1966.

*MASAKAZU YAMAZAKI, b. 1934
Playwright and Professor of Theater Studies, Osaka University
A lecturer, professor, playwright, and critic, Mr. Yamazaki has had his plays produced in New York, St. Louis, and Florence, Italy, as well as in Japan. Best known abroad for his plays *Zeami* and *Sanetomo,* he is also the author of literary essays on Mori Ogai and on the tenor of the times. A graduate of Kyoto University, he spent a year at the Yale School of Drama and has been Visiting Professor of Modern Japanese Intellectual History at Columbia University. Pro-

fessor Yamazaki won the Kishida Prize for New Playwrights (1963) and the National Festival Award (1974).

Discussant: Donald Keene, author, translator, and Professor of Japanese Literature, Columbia University.

PANEL 4
The Japanese Economy in the World

*YOTARO KOBAYASHI, b. 1933
President, Fuji Xerox
Mr. Kobayashi joined Fuji Photo Film Company in 1958, after receiving his B.A. in economics from Keio University and M.B.A. from The Wharton School. In 1963 he was assigned to Fuji Xerox, where he was director and manager of marketing, planning, and publicity. He rose through the marketing operations division to become president of the firm in 1978.

KAZUO NUKAZAWA, b. 1936
Senior Assistant Director, Economic Cooperation Department, Keidanren (Federation of Economic Organizations)
A specialist on world economics, Mr. Nukazawa joined Keidanren in 1959 after graduating from Hitotsubashi University. The author of *Restructurization of French Industry* and co-author of *The French Economy, Today and Tomorrow* (both in Japanese), he has written many articles on balance of trade, foreign investment, and economic conflict. A member of government and private missions to Latin America and Asia, he has spent considerable time in the United States as well, doing research on economics at the U.S.–Japan Trade Council and the Rockefeller Foundation.

*EISUKE SAKAKIBARA, b. 1941
Associate Professor of Economics, Saitama University
Professor Sakakibara was with the Ministry of Finance for ten years, rising to Deputy Director of the Banking Bureau. He is the author of numerous articles on balance of payments and Eurocurrency. He was educated at the University of Tokyo and the University of Michigan, where he completed a Ph.D. in Economics in 1969.

Discussants: Paul Finney, Executive Editor, *Fortune;* Hugh Patrick, Professor of Economics, Yale University.

PANEL 5
Politics in Japan

*TASUKU ASANO, b. 1936
Professor of Political Science, International College of Commerce
and Economics, Tokyo, and anchorman, NEWSCOPE evening
news, Tokyo Broadcasting System
A specialist on American party and electoral politics, Professor
Asano has written articles on American politics, presidential campaigns, and foreign relations for *Asahi Journal, Ekonomisto,* and *Toyo
Keizai Shinpo.* He has translated into Japanese Roger Hilsman's *To
Move a Nation* and David Halberstam's *The Best and the Brightest.* Educated at Tokyo University of Foreign Studies and Columbia University's School of International Affairs, he was a Fulbright Scholar at
the University of Pennsylvania in 1963.

YOSHIO MURAKAMI, b. 1937
Foreign correspondent, *Asahi Shimbun*
Mr. Murakami joined the *Asahi Shimbun* as a specialist on U.S.–Japan
relations in 1966. He covered the reversion of the Bonin Islands, the
1968 presidential election, and the Saigon peace talks. From 1973 to
1975 he was bureau chief in Bangkok. He served as the *Asahi's*
Washington and White House correspondent from 1975 to 1979. In
1977, Mr. Murakami was awarded the Japan Newspaper Association Award for his coverage of the Lockheed scandal. He was educated at Keio University and the Fletcher School of Law and
Diplomacy, where he received his Ph.D. in 1964.

*KAN ORI, b. 1933
Professor of Political Science, Sophia University
Professor Ori has written extensively on politics, parties, and public
opinion and has lectured at colleges and universities in the United
States and Europe. Educated in the United States, he received his
Ph.D. in Political Science from Indiana University in 1961. His latest
publication is *Political Parties, Elites, and Conflict Resolution in Japanese
Politics,* co-authored with Roger Benjamin.

Discussants: George Packard, Woodrow Wilson International Center
for Scholars; Herbert Passin, Professor of Sociology, Columbia University; Bernard Silberman, Professor of Political Science, University of Chicago.

PANEL 6
Issues of Urban Society

RYOHEI KAKUMOTO, b. 1920
Board of Directors, Japan Transport Economics Research Center,
and Visiting Professor, Waseda University
Dr. Kakumoto, who received his B.A. from the University of Tokyo
and his Ph.D. from Osaka University of Commerce, was with the
Japan National Railways from 1941 to 1970. Following his retire-
ment he has been the author of several books, including *Man,
Transportation, and the City* and *Contemporary Transport Policy.* Dr.
Kakumoto has served as a member of the management committee
of the Tokyo Rapid Transit Authority and of the cabinet-level
Railways Construction Council.

HIDETOSHI KATO, b. 1930
Director, Research Institute for Oriental Cultures, Gakushuin Uni-
versity, and Research Associate, Communications Institute, East-
West Center
Professor Kato, the author of more than twenty books and articles,
has recently completed a comparative study of "street life" in
Tokyo, Hong Kong, and Manila and is currently doing research on
the history of media in Japan. He has lectured, taught, or done
research at Harvard University, the University of Chicago, Grinnell
College, and the University of Kent. A graduate of Hitotsubashi
University, Professor Kato received his Ph.D. from Toyo University.

FUMIHIKO MAKI, b. 1928
Architect, Maki and Associates, and Lecturer, Department of Urban
Engineering, University of Tokyo
A winner of Japanese and international awards and citations for his
designs, Mr. Maki has planned housing complexes, sports facilities,
and public buildings, including the National Museum of Modern
Art in Kyoto and the Rissho University Kumagaya Campus, for
which he received the Mainichi Art Award. A lecturer, author, and
critic, he has taught or spoken at Harvard University, University of
California at Berkeley, Columbia University, and University of California at Los Angeles, among others. Educated at the University of
Tokyo and Harvard University, his first position was with Skid-
more, Owings, and Merrill. His publications include *Metabolism 1960*
and *What Is Urban Space?* co-authored with Noboru Kawazoe.

Discussants: Tetsuo Najita, Professor of History, University of Chicago; Robert Reischauer, Congressional Budget Office.

1 2 3 4 5 6 7 8 9 10 11 12 13   90 89 88 87 86 85 84 83 82 81